C000080446

245

Ignition!

Ignition!

Sparking
Organizational Change

Rani Chaudhry-Lawton

and

Richard Lawton

CENTURY
BUSINESS

Copyright © Rani Chaudhry-Lawton & Richard Lawton 1992

The right of Rani Chaudhry-Lawton and Richard Lawton to be identified as the authors of this work has been asserted by them in accordance with the Copyright, Designs and Patents Act 1988

First published in Great Britain in 1992 by
Century Business
An imprint of Random Century Limited
20 Vauxhall Bridge Road, London SW1V 2SA

Random Century Australia (Pty) Limited
20 Alfred Street, Milsons Point, Sydney
New South Wales 2061, Australia

Random Century New Zealand Limited
18 Poland Road, Glenfield
Auckland 10, New Zealand

Random Century South Africa (Pty) Limited
PO Box 337, Bergvlei, South Africa

Set in Baskerville by 🄰 Tek Art Ltd, Addiscombe, Croydon, Surrey
Printed and bound in Great Britain by

British Library Cataloguing in Publication Data
A catalogue record for this book is available from the British Library

ISBN 0-7126-9821-3

Companies, institutions and other organizations wishing to make bulk purchases of this title or any other Century Business publication should contact:

Direct Sales Manager
Century Business
Random Century House
20 Vauxhall Bridge Road
London SW1V 2SA

Fax: 071-828 6681

Contents

FOR SHARIF – OUR FAVOURITE SPARK

Foreword

One constant factor has run all the way through my working life, from the time that I left school and put to sea as a cadet purser, through my days with the Hertz and Avis car rental companies in Europe and the United States, then with the Sears retail group in London and subsequently during my time at British Airways.

That constant, paradoxically as it may sound, is change.

The future holds many uncertainties, but looking ahead there is one thing of which I am sure. Change – and, once again, excuse me if I appear to contradict myself – is here to stay.

I will go further than that. Change is going to come about ever faster and more frequently.

I base that assertion not on any private crystal ball, Tarot cards or favourite piece of seaweed, but on recent trends in my own working life and in the world as a whole.

Improvements in technology and communications are altering our perspectives. What was high-tech yesterday is commonplace today and will be obsolete tomorrow. The world is becoming increasingly 'local', with events more frequently having an immediate impact on a global level. The more we experience – and progress means we are all experiencing more and more – so too do our expectations grow.

Greater variety is becoming available in virtually every sphere of life.

Increasingly commonly, at work and at leisure, people are being confronted by situations they have never before experienced, whether it is simply the latest in fast-changing fashion fads or, more seriously, the implications for your home market of a plummeting collapse in share prices in a country 8,000 miles away.

In industry and commerce, as a result, laid-down procedures on how to deal with standard occurrences are becoming increasingly redundant.

A company has to be sufficiently flexible to be able to adapt to differing requirements and circumstances, and to take advantage of new ideas and possibilities, from the boardroom to the shop floor.

From my own experience, many find this uncomfortable, even daunting, at first. However, once they get used to the concept, they find it can make life more exciting and enjoyable.

What it means to business is quite clear to me. Those who are best able to manage change have the best prospects for success. Those who are unable to manage change are unlikely to survive.

Ignition! Sparking Organizational Change provides managers with a first class guide to get ahead in the change process.

Sir Colin Marshall
Deputy Chairman and Chief
Executive of British Airways

Acknowledgements

When we wrote *Ignition!* we were in the happy position of being able to find an ideal atmosphere for researching, thinking and writing. Most of the first draft of the book was written during a sabbatical taken in Park City in the American Rockies. While the snow fell on the Wasatch Front, as our part of the world was known, we read and wrote and when it had settled, we skied.

Support for our book (the Air, in terms of our model) came from a number of people and it is to them that we like to offer our warmest thanks. We are grateful to our clients and the many managers who have contributed ideas and helped to clarify our thinking. Specifically we would like to thank Chris Swan and Brian Hamill for their very early support for *Ignition!* and particularly for Spark groups. They provided us with an ideal *Ignition!* project and helped to advance our thinking considerably through debate and discussion. A group of people in Park City helped us in practical ways and gave us plenty of encouragement. Shirley Miller provided us with a superb house during our stay and our good friends Larry and Sandra Thacker guided us through some of the mysteries of living in a small town in the heart of Mormon Utah (we now know what a cord of wood is, for example). Lisa Cilva, who herself was studying part-time in the area of organizational change, encouraged us directly and by her own example of diligence and effort. We benefited greatly from the comments of a succession of visitors to our Park City home and in particular, those of our parents, John and Gwen Lawton, who were willingly persuaded to do some proof reading.

Throughout our stay, we were posting our scribbled manuscripts back to England where Ann Butler interpreted the writing and put the finished product on to the word processor. Our thanks to her for getting us started and to a team of Mara Consultants' administrators who typed the re-drafts: Vicky Smith, Sara Higgison, Paula Yau and Caroline Gray. Perhaps the least enviable task fell to our current P.A. Debbie Dudley who has had the job of ensuring that the final version is on one word processing system and in one place where it can be retrieved. We are especially grateful to her for her patience with the closing stages.

Having kindled the spark of interest with our publishers, we have been very well served by Elizabeth Hennessy and Martin Liu at Century Business. Particularly helpful, as always, has been the marketing advice we have received from Virginia Merritt. Stimulated by the many authors we read during our research, we have used a large number of quotes in the book and our thanks go to Lisa Stolerman for helping us to obtain the necessary permissions.

It is not possible to thank mountains in the same way as people, so we will conclude with an acknowledgement of the superb environment for writing provided by the background of the Utah Rockies.

Rani Chaudhry-Lawton
Richard Lawton

Introduction

'*In skating over thin ice, our safety is in our speed*'. Ralph Waldo Emerson

At a recent conference for middle and senior managers we sampled a cross-section of the conversations that took place during the lunch break. The snatches of people's hopes, fears and plans made fascinating listening. The following will serve as an illustration.

A. *They were superb. I took a big risk taking that secondment out to Hong Kong and I thought they would leave me in limbo when the situation changed there and they had to call me back early. Instead of that, they asked me to head up a new area devoted to opening up our markets in the Pacific Basin.*

B. *They used to come to us, cap in hand and we'd sit back for a while, scratch our foreheads and decide whether or not we were going to do any lending. Now we're providing counselling, for free. Some of my older managers think that counselling is something only done by therapists.*

C. *It's a whole new pattern of negotiation and consultation. The staff side has just agreed to our proposals for flexible working without the usual fight over quid pro quos. They even came up with some bright ideas themselves. Now our industrial relations advisers are panicking because they don't know what to do with their spare time.*

D. *We are ideally placed to go into Europe but we're paralysed because no one knows anything about it. The half that haven't got the languages are waiting for it to go away and the half that have are too afraid to use them. I've got some enthusiasts in our information management department so I think they're going to have to lead the way for the rest of them.*

E. *The growing number of people who are into these specialist hobbies gives us an ideal opportunity for a new product range. I've offered it to the company and if they don't want it, I'm thinking of doing it myself, anyway. I'll set up on my own if I have to.*

All these delegates whose conversations we have quoted were obviously sharing the experience of change. These took various forms such as a fresh opportunity, a discomforting shift in direction of the company, new behaviours being demanded, fear of something different and the excitement of a creative idea. What they didn't share, however, was a common reaction to what was happening. It doesn't take too much imagination to picture which situations might have led quickly to productive change and which might have remained stuck for some time. From an organizational point of view it is critical that all the excitement, fear, restlessness, curiosity and panic that surrounds change should be focused into productive and enjoyable activity. It is critical from an individual point of view also. Most people like to feel that they are in charge of their lives, which on many occasions means taking the initiative rather than being pushed around by the consequences of change initiated by others. This book is written for all those managers within organizations who have been given the responsibility of responding to new developments or initiating change themselves. Our aim is to stimulate thought and provide guidance, for people who are part of the type of change which needs to be high impact, swift and which very probably needs to move out of the way before the next change comes along.

In writing a book about change, we have chosen to try to capture some of the excitement and energy that accompanies the swift and radical nature of the transformations that are sweeping a number of organizations both in the private and public sectors. We have chosen to focus, therefore, on the kind of change that will set an organization alight, as opposed to warming it up slightly, hence our metaphor of Ignition. In writing about Ignition we have drawn on our experience of being managers and our experience of being consultants to describe what it is like. At the same time, we have also liberally sprinkled the text with advice about how to achieve it.

It is not our intention to analyse all the aspects of change, as that has been well done elsewhere. We are, however, interested in three particular features which characterize present day change and which we believe demand the type of response that we refer to as Ignition. As time progresses, change becomes more invasive: it is in our homes and workplaces whether we like it or not. The rate of change is rapid and it is increasing. Its third feature is that it has a random quality which adds to its capacity to excite and shock.

We have tried to provide a simple outline for what we believe to be the main elements of Ignition and have labelled these ingredients, Fuel, Air and Spark. The manager in example E, for instance, had clearly been stimulated by what she detected as changing patterns in the leisure market and this prompted some ideas of her own. The ideas and outside stimuli we refer to as Fuel. For the manager in example A, the thing that impressed him about his own company was the fact that he took a risk in accepting a secondment and that it had supported him when the move didn't work out because the situation had changed in Hong Kong. Support in many different forms (attention, resources, time and training) is a vital element in organizational change and we have labelled this ingredient Air. The Spark element is the third ingredient and represents the behaviour of an individual or group that is aimed at giving the new development a push, a commitment of energy or a way around an obstacle. If our manager in example E had decided to promote her idea either within the organization or for her own benefit, it would be the Spark element that would make the difference between a good idea and action. We can only speculate as to whether the information management department in example D was enthusiastic enough actually to provide the Spark necessary to lead the way for the rest of them. Before looking at these elements in more detail, in the following chapters of the book, it is worth looking at some of the features of change that give both individuals and organizations a challenge.

The invasive nature of change is well illustrated by the impact of television. Setting aside the debate about its capacity to produce imitative behaviour following screenings of violence, its ability to land us in the centre of major events is very powerful. It is now a few years since the Challenger space shuttle exploded in full view of millions across the world who were watching television. Even now it is a powerful memory for many Americans who had switched on their sets in the expectation of seeing an historical news item and instead witnessed a personal and national tragedy.

A century ago, a disease such as Aids could have been expected to remain in Africa or the West Coast of America for some time before being detected in rural English villages; not so today. Until the advent of nuclear power, Cumbrian sheep farmers would have put the introduction of foot and mouth disease by pedestrian visitors highest on the list of undesirable invasions. Even after the introduction of nuclear power it would have been hard for them to predict the threat posed by a Soviet nuclear power plant, half way across the world, whose failure in 1986 placed an airborne mega-pollutant in their own fields.

The more forward-thinking corporations have already come to grips with the rapid pace of change. Naisbitt and Aburdene refer to one of the Japanese giants which had majored in home electric appliances since 1918 now throwing all its efforts behind semiconductors, telecommunications and information-related equipment. As a number of observers have pointed out, product life cycles in many areas are getting much shorter and the two or three decades that it would have taken the home appliances to reach market maturity will be replaced by information technology products reaching maturity in well under a decade. For example, before the compact disc market has had the chance to mature, the D.A.T. (Digital Audio Tape) threatens to nudge it out of the way. This shortening of the product life cycle has produced a radical response on the part of the company, which is now deliberately scrapping semiconducting manufacturing equipment each year in order to stay at the leading edge. It is prepared to sacrifice the high cost and the loss of tax advantage (Japanese tax laws allow depreciation over five years) in exchange for being in the forefront.

Charles Handy makes the useful observation that we do not currently have a suitable way of reckoning the potential for depreciation in the skills and knowledge of our human resource. This suggests an interesting 'thought experiment' in which we imagine an individual manager or specialist 'depreciating' over a period of years. If a semiconductor manufacturing plant can depreciate over five years, then so can people. In fact we have met several people in organizations who, by virtue of having done no learning or development over a period of time, can be said to have seriously depreciated their talents relative to the new tasks and challenges that confront them. Organizations might be lucky in that their managers and specialists may learn almost accidentally, just by doing a new job. Some take this as an excuse for doing no or very little off-the-job training. The Japanese example above, if extended to the human resource area, would have very radical implications. It would effectively mean re-equipping employees each year with all the new skills and knowledge that they would need for the forthcoming year.

Perhaps change would require less effort and managing if it were a bit more predictable. Straight line extrapolations of current trends into the future have a habit of falling flat on their faces. Those who attempt such extrapolations, referred to by Naisbitt as the 'gee-whizz furturists' fail to see the randomness interwoven in the process and fail to see that change 'weaves and bobs and lurches and splutters'. In one well known example, a group of futurists at the turn of the century coupled the projected population growth with the use of horse-drawn transport in London and predicted streets waist deep in manure. Any of them alive today would have to come to grips with the fact that a four-wheel machine has rendered horse-drawn transport obsolete, and not only that, it can be powered using the methane gas from animal manure that they feared would be choking London.

The random aspect of change comes in a number of forms. In the case of international terrorism, the random factor is inherent in the intentions of the terrorists to cause maximum shock. For the individual manager working in any one of a number of areas in the air travel industry, even the indirect impact of a terrorist attack on his/her everyday experience of handling change, is likely to feel very random indeed. The destruction of the Pan Am flight over Lockerbie, besides causing immense human loss and misery to those immediately involved, undoubtedly caused upheaval at a far more mundane level. It does not take much imagination to picture the impact on those responsible for airport security, explosive detection experts, aircraft construction specialists, public relations employees and a host of related functions. Random happenings on this scale have a habit of attracting other problems in the attendant glare of publicity and adding to the feeling of change as an invasive process, as referred to earlier. The press was quick to pick up the stories of people who gained illegal access to aircraft and filmed themselves doing it. After a police exercise to train drug sniffing dogs, one of the sample packets was left behind on an aeroplane and went undetected for some considerable time. When it was discovered, it attracted a lot of media attention.

Sometimes a cluster of factors suddenly conspire to pose a problem. 1986 saw a bombing in La Belle, a West Berlin discotheque popular with U.S. servicemen, the hijacking of the *Achille Lauro* and Ronald Reagan's decision to bomb Colonel Gaddafi's residence and headquarters using the UK as a base. These incidents, together with the shower of deadly radioactive fallout released by the Chernobyl power plant in the USSR, made European travel suddenly very unattractive to a number of American citizens. A number of them toughed it out with tee-shirts proclaiming 'I survived Europe 1986'. There were not sufficient numbers of optimistic American humorists, however, to keep transatlantic flights full. This clearly posed a threat to British Airways, in its pre-privatization build up. It responded swiftly with its 'Go for it America' campaign, a successful attempt to win back lost passengers by an up-beat marketing exercise on American soil. The word 'swiftly' is important here because British Airways could not have predicted the need for such an intensive campaign and in fact had to mount it in the face of a significant body of criticism, and commit a significant amount of resource to it in a short space of time.

There are other changes destined to affect business and the general public which also seem like a random spanner in the works but which in fact creep up rather than descending overnight. The insurance industry has been reaping the harvest of seeds sown some decades previously. It took a long time for the full effects of the use of asbestos in construction to be appreciated. The long-term effects of the particularly toxic defoliant, Agent Orange (used by the Americans to reduce enemy cover during the Vietnam War) were such that a group of Vietnam War veterans, who had been in contact with it, were claiming for damages as late as the 1980s. Insurance companies found that they had underwritten risks which may have looked reasonable twenty or thirty years previously but which began to appear very large and threatening by the 1970s and 1980s. Such is the pace of scientific innovation that in the case of Agent Orange, help may be at hand, as scientists have discovered a microbe that will feed on one of its core constituents. The power of research into herbicides, which initially produced the problem, now seems to have come full circle as it works towards a solution.

Even a phenomenon as well documented as the Aids virus still has the capacity to surprise. Following the news that one out of every 61 infants born in New York City tested HIV positive (and so has an estimated 40 per cent chance of developing the full-blown Aids disease) State Health Commissioner David Axelrod commented: 'What is alarming is that this is a higher level of infection that we had considered to be likely within the overall community'. It will clearly continue to produce shocks for future generations as Aids may not reveal itself for as long as a decade ('The Aids epidemic of the late 1990s has already happened', according to one expert.) Until relatively recently, many people did not take seriously the capacity of Aids to spread through the heterosexual as well as the homosexual community. The announcement by Earvin 'Magic' Johnson, the American basketball star, that he is HIV positive, has stunned many of his fans. His affairs with a succession of women had been an open secret but its significance had not struck people until his announcement.

In the face of change which is, as described above, invasive, very fast and random, individuals and organizations may make a number of responses. Two of the more negative responses would be active resistance and temporary rejection. Active resistance of change requires a tremendous amount of commitment and energy. Even some of the more determined individuals and communities find the enemy constantly at their gates. The Amish community in the USA in many ways maintain an attractive adherence to the work ethic and a strong moral framework, with rejection of power-driven technologies. They can be seen in their own traditional dress, riding horse-drawn buggies and also using horses to plough the land. However, national economic forces such as high interest rates and comparatively poor returns from agriculture have seriously affected the community. For the first time, the Church has recently decided to give the men permission to take jobs as carpenters in nearby towns.

Even geographically and socially isolated people such as the people of Kau in East Africa are not immune from the invasive nature of outside influence. Their ancestry dates back to the Nubians of ancient history. Some of this history can be seen demonstrated in the warrior contest rituals of the men and body and scarification rituals of the women. However, in the middle of these most ancient of ceremonies, a proudly worn pair of sunglasses can often plainly be seen. Ironically, perhaps, one of the first intrusions into an isolated culture may well be the anthropologists who intend only to observe and who may later become the champions of an attempt to preserve the culture. Yet the anthropologists bring their own culture with them and start the change process.

In organizational settings there are some people who see their role in life as resisting change. Unless they are large in number, or sitting on large amounts of power, their more innovative colleagues will usually find a way of getting round the obstacle they present. This may take varying forms ranging from direct action with its attendant risk of a showdown with the person involved or, less explicitly, operating in a different part of the organization where support is more forthcoming. Sometimes a whole organization may be dominated by actively change resistant managers. The reason these organizations exist at all is probably a function of the reserves that they have managed to build up over past years or the fact that their industry has only recently caught the eye of some sharp competitors.

Slightly more common than the active resistance phenomenon is the temporary rejection of change. In its crudest form it is expressed in a desire to wait until the latest fancy fashion or flavour of the month passes over what is usually deemed to be the 'sharp end' of the business. One door-to-door selling organization in the UK changed its strategy and tactics so often that it actually benefited its middle management to hold back from committing to the latest development. In the midst of their understandable cynicism, however, what the managers failed to see was that the woods were indeed burning and some form of radical adaptation would be essential.

Perhaps a more subtle form of the temporary rejection of change is expressed in the phrase 'there is nothing new under the sun'. Some of the wise elders in the organization will point out that they have 'seen it all before' when faced with a new policy from management. They will use the pendulum argument of swings from 'a' to 'b' then back to 'a' again. Unfortunately this argument, which has some superficial attraction, is often used to kill a new development or idea. In one organization a new performance review system was likened to the management by objectives scheme attempted some ten years previously ('and we all know *that* didn't work!').

What negates this argument is the fact that even if familiar change themes apear to crop up at intervals, they do so in radically changed circumstances. British Rail chose to phase out the luxury Pullman coaches that were part of some of their long-distance services. A more recent shift in the marketing philosophy has led British Rail to re-introduce the Pullman coaches. However, a ride in a Pullman today pulled by a swift Inter-City diesel is a very different proposition from a ride in a Pullman in the days of steam. Quite apart from the journey itself the whole concept of rail transport has altered in the intervening years. A greatly reduced network, the expansion of the motorway system and cheap internal flights have all had their impact on rail policy. Under the recent Tory administrations there have even been mutterings of privatization. Again, the cynic may see in this move an attempt to capture the pre-nationalization days of a regional rail service. There may be some superficial similarities, but our cynic would now have to add into the equation the possible impact of superconductivity on rail transport technology and the significance of a rail link through the Channel Tunnel.

Pascale and Athos analyse the approach of Matsushita (corporate head of the giant that produces National, Panasonic and Technics) to the 'unresolvable conflict of centralization versus decentralization'. Thus 1945 to 1952 sees central control, 1953-55 decentralization and 1955-1960 a swing to recentralization. The significant thing about these moves, however, is that they occur in response to and have impact on, a much changed environment. Hence the postwar centralization is a response to the turmoil and recession of the period but the need for flexibility during a period of increased customer choice in the early 50s led to decentralization. The move back to central control corresponded with a period of high growth and penetration of international markets. A change cynic observing Matsushita's example might only see the switches from one policy back to the original one and miss the significance of the altered circumstances to which he was responding.

It can reduce a lot of the anxiety surrounding change to have as a central philosophy the idea that things will soon return to normal. One of our clients had undergone some painful transitions when it formed one large organization by the merger of two medium-sized ones. The new organization had found itself still uncompetitive and had implemented radical improvements on all fronts, one of which was a series of corporate programmes aimed at enhancing customer and competitor awareness. We had just completed a training course for some of the discussion leaders in the newest of these corporate events. One of our older participants, who still identified with his original company, pre-merger, came up to us at the end of the programme, beaming from ear to ear and said, 'Great course, you know, it really reminded me of the old days.' Having worked very hard to bury without trace the old regime, with its hierarchies, bureaucracies and complete lack of customer awareness, we were rather shocked by his comment. On sober reflection, we decided to take it as a compliment because the 'old days' were clearly held in such high regard by the participant, and we just had to hope that he was referring to the team spirit that he had enjoyed in times gone by.

Our main interest in this book is not how to tackle the problems of active resistance or temporary rejection of change. What we will do is to concentrate on looking at ways in which individuals, groups and organizations can get on with changes that they know they need to make with energy, enthusiasm, speed and success. This is the wholehearted, committed type of change that we labelled Ignition, earlier in the chapter. That does not mean that we are denying the problems that resistance can create and we touch on them briefly in the chapter 'There Has to Be a Better Way' when we look at the problems of mild acceptance, finding a scapegoat and 'tuning-out'. Generally, however, we are keen to take a more positive viewpoint and starting with the assumption that many individuals and organizations want to make change happen, we address the question of how to do that more effectively.

The book is divided into three sections. Sections I and II ('The Air/Fuel Mixture' and 'Generating Sparks') look at the condition necessary for Ignition. The third Section ('Some Guidelines for Ignition') is designed to give guidance to those wanting to implement some of the principles outlined earlier in the book.

The Air/Fuel Mixture Section is focused mainly at the organizational level, because it is at this level that the support (Air) and the innovative ideas or responses (Fuel) necessary for Ignition, usually occur. Our analysis of Sparks, however, is pitched at the level of the individual and the group. We are using the term Sparks to encompass a wide range of behaviours which we believe helps to make change take off, given the right mix of Air and Fuel.

In an ideal world, it might be possible for an individual Spark to be capable of all the behaviours identified in the 'Generating Sparks' section. That would probably be too much to ask, however, as the different sorts of behaviour embrace a wide variety of interpersonal and cognitive styles. More realistically, we can expect different Sparks to have different talents such as overcoming an obstacle or being quick to read the signposts in a changed environment. For this reason it is important to acknowledge the importance that a group of people can have in promoting organizational change. This is partly because of the mix of styles and partly because of the added strength of greater numbers. Throughout the book we have referred to instances of the Spark element of Ignition coming from a team as well as from an individual.

There are two chapters devoted to generating Sparks ('Change Really is Change' and 'There Has to Be a Better Way'). Each chapter itself encompasses a range of Spark-like behaviour. In the 'Change Really is Change' chapter, we emphasize the importance of recognizing that circumstances have actually altered, the importance of reading the signposts and knowing when they have shifted. 'There Has to Be a Better Way' describes the Spark in action, overcoming obstacles by tackling them head on, by acting with bursts of energy or by breaking the rules in maverick fashion.

It is with the Spark that our main interest in the change process lies, that is, with the activist individual or group who has the energy to push through a new development. We have placed little emphasis on the need for careful diagnosis as part of a change initiative. This is partly because it has been well documented elsewhere but mainly because we wish to de-emphasize its importance. Traditional models of organizational change give diagnosis a central role. However, in view of the speed and randomness which we believe accompanies many new developments, it is our view that long diagnostic phases may become redundant or positively obstructive. The Spark deliberately risks an incomplete diagnosis in favour of taking action. In doing so, he/she may make some mistakes but will rarely miss an opportunity through being too slow.

As practitioners in the organization change field, it is almost impossible for us not to make recommendations as we go along and we have not tried to avoid doing this. We have devoted a section purely to advice ('Some Guidelines for Ignition'). All three chapters in this section are 'how to' chapters. 'Beyond Vision' acknowledges the role played by creating ideal pictures of the future but goes on to stress the essential qualities of being able to get support for a vision, of keeping the commitment alive and following through to ensure that desired actions happen. 'Start Somewhere' gives guidance on the different ways to get change moving and 'Spark Groups' highlights the ways in which teams can be used to promote

Ignition. In addition we have summarized the tips and hints at the end of each chapter (Flashpoints).

This introduction opened with a series of examples of a number of different individuals who were facing a new development, challenge or possibly threat. It is our belief that the way in which people choose to approach their change situations is an organizational as well as an individual issue. Given the nature of change as we have described it in this chapter it is also our belief that both individuals and organizations need an appropriate response to what confronts them. In our terms, that means leading or becoming part of, Ignition.

REFERENCES

- Naisbitt, J. and Aburdene, P. (1985) *Re-inventing the Corporation,* New York: Warner Books.

- Handy, C.B. (1976) *Understanding Organizations,* Harmondsworth: Penguin Books.

- Naisbitt, J. (1984) *Megatrends*, New York: Warner Books.

- Brown, A. and Weiner, E. (1984) *Supermanaging,* New York: McGraw-Hill

- *'Plague of the Innocents'* Time January 1988.

- Riefenstahl, L. (1976) *People of Kau,* (English translation) London: William Collins.

- Pascale, R.T. and Athos, A.G. (1981) *The Art of Japanese Management,* New York: Warner Books.

- *Bloomsbury Dictionary of Quotations,* (1987) Bloomsbury Publishing Ltd.

Section I

The Air/Fuel Mixture

1. The Air/Fuel Mixture

'The amount a person uses his imagination is inversely proportional to the amount of punishment he will receive for using it.'   (Roger Von Oech)

'They want a cat that barks and we can't even miaow.'
(A puzzled manager contemplating yet another organizational change)

'I'm not worried about the long term so much in this particular instance. I am trying to make sure the initiative has plenty of oxygen and energy over the next 12 months.'   (Sir John Egan, Chief Executive, BAA)

Air, which represents the different forms of atmosphere in which change takes place and Fuel, which represents the ideas and stimuli which drive the change forward, are both vitally important. Our aim in this chapter is to highlight different aspects of the Air/Fuel mixture. More importantly, we integrate the different types of Air and Fuel in a model which serves as a means of looking at four different types of organizational response to the change question.

AIR

If change is to happen, the individuals, groups and organizations pushing it forward have to be able to breathe. As a bare minimum, the key people involved need some of the barriers and obstacles to their ideas and actions to be removed. However, this really is a bare minimum and for a new development to take off rapidly and successfully there ideally needs to be an atmosphere of positive support and encouragement. This suggests a range of atmosphere along the Air dimension, from Weak to Strong.

WEAK AIR

In this case the organization's message to the individual or group with an idea or a new development appears to be something along the lines of, 'Fine, we won't stop you but you realize this will have to be done in your own time.'

In one episode, some colleagues of ours had taken on a huge project. It involved the selection of a complete tier of management using a method based on the model often referred to as an Assessment Centre. As is the case with some training courses, a group of participants, taken away from the workplace, take part in a series of leaderless group discussions, case studies and psychometric tests. The main difference is that the information produced by an Assessment Centre is used to make a selection decision or to suggest a programme of future development.

Our colleagues had done a professional job in designing the Assessment Centre, but they were, of necessity, very complex processes. They were residential and were an administrative nightmare. Each day ran to a very tight schedule requiring co-ordination of candidates and the Assessment Panel. Each stage of the process from application through assessment to final feedback, involved large amounts of paper. Our colleagues threw themselves wholeheartedly into the project for a variety of motives. They gained genuine professional satisfaction from a job thoroughly executed, they wanted to raise their visibility and credibility in the organization and they hoped for increased remuneration. The increased remuneration would go some way towards compensating for the ridiculous number of hours that they were working and the prolonged absences from home. Although they gained the professional satisfaction, visibility and credibility that they were seeking, their increased remuneration was denied to them in a fairly brutal fashion. At the end of the project they approached their boss with their case only to hear from him the words, 'No one asked you to put in the extra hours'. This meeting and the ensuing period of demotivation had a dramatic effect on the group for several months afterwards.

A few years ago Apple Macintosh Computers ran an advertisement on British television. It featured a head of department poring over high resolution computer graphics while several floors down, their creators walk smartly into the building carrying their own home computers. He catches sight of the men entering the building and asks his assistant what they are carrying. There is visible shock on his face when he learns that they have used their own (Apple Macintosh) computers to produce the graphics because the company's computers were not up to scratch. The final shot is of a grim-faced head of department ordering his assistant to get hold of an Apple Macintosh.

In the case of the Apple advertisement, the men who have produced the high resolution graphics presumably have enough initiative to go their own way. If an organization is to grow, beat the competition and innovate, it cannot rely on its employees always having enough drive to be effective in a poor atmosphere. A manager of a training department in a large multi-site organization used to bemoan the fact that his senior management hardly ever gave him direction and guidance and certainly never provided any clues as to how they saw management training fitting into the corporate strategy. For long enough, he continued undaunted and he and his team innovated in many different areas. Senior management rarely objected or presented obstacles but neither did they offer active support. Eventually their extremely half-hearted relationship with training led to the disillusionment of the manager and the team. The majority of individuals left the company and now hold down top human resources appointments with other organizations and consultancies or run their own businesses.

An organization with an atmosphere of Weak Air will find that it is driving the more able and innovative individuals to leave and find new outlets for their energies. Naisbitt and Aburdene quote the example of California's Hank Heeber, the owner of four tyre stores, three shoe stores and a cattle ranch, who once increased the profit of his employer, a retailer, by $100,000. His 'reward' was a pay rise of $50 per month, which so insulted him that he immediately left. Companies who have really grasped the importance of preventing this from happening actively encourage the person with budding entrepreneurial talents to operate within the organization (the section on Strong Air looks at the way in which this can be done).

Monetary compensation is not always the issue at stake when it comes to assessing whether the atmosphere is a supportive one or not. In the case of one company that introduced a new promotional grade and accompanying assessment system, the impact of the managers' support became crucial. Not only did the increased promotional opportunities destabilize the expectations of those managers who wanted to cruise for a few years in their jobs before contemplating promotion, but also the nature of the selection made the winners and losers very visible indeed. Coupled with the fact that each candidate came back from the Assessment Centre with detailed feedback on his or her performance, the attempt at promotion suddenly became a very stressful and risky business. This new system was introduced into the company with very little warning and certainly no attempt to allay fears or even sell the concept.

The 'failures' of the system went one of three ways. They either rallied and re-applied for a second Assessment Centre, sought counselling, or they waged private guerilla warfare on the organization. Help through counselling was in short supply and was not something that the company had thought to prepare for in advance. The net result was that more than was necessary of the failed managers who had taken the decision badly, joined the guerillas. In one region a group of guerillas banded together to form a club which had as its emblem a tie proudly announcing 'We failed the 1981 Assessment Centre.' More details of this case are provided in *Opportunities and Threats* in the chapter 'Change Really is Change' (see page 52).

Psychological support is not just about the need for a sympathetic ear, as in the above example. Feedback generally, both positive and negative, is an important part of the individual's support system. It is true that constant negative feedback is likely either to grind a person down or produce a crisis, but perhaps a more usual failing is a complete absence of feedback. Ironically enough, it is a phenomenon reported very often by those who are in a position of power during organizational change. From our own experience, we know that many top executives experience isolation from good quality feedback about their own competence and standing within the company. Moss Kanter describes it when she says 'In one multi-national corporation, top executives who are sealed off in a large distant office, flattered and virtually babied by aides, are frustrated by their distance from the real action.'

Chief Executives and Feedback Starvation

In one survey conducted by the Centre for Creative Leadership, North Carolina, four important factors emerged as reasons why many top executives experienced feedback starvation. These were identified as being the executives' demeanour, exaggerated impact, isolation and relative autonomy.

The executives' demeanour may have a number of different aspects. For some chief executives there is an aura of mystique surrounding them before they actually do anything. If they choose to add to this by talking in a very dominant and competitive fashion or by being actively abrasive, then the distancing effect which is already present becomes amplified. Subordinates may be reluctant to give feedback if they will have to compete to get a word in edgeways or, worse still, if they suspect they will receive the rough edge of the chief executive's tongue. In several organizations, the chief executive is regarded as having a great deal of power, sometimes way beyond his/her actual intentions. Thus a throwaway comment might be seized on by subordinates as a significant policy statement. Taken to extreme, subordinates may constantly try to provide their leader with a flow of support and good news. In this environment, very little useful feedback, and certainly no negative feedback, is likely to reach the chief executive's ears.

Other factors removing chief executives from realistic feedback are the comparative isolation in which they often exist and their autonomy. There will be greater isolation in organizations with several hierarchical layers where contact with the rest of the company may be mainly through a handful of senior executives who are also isolated. Autonomy can be an isolating factor if top executives use it to hire people who confirm their own views and stereotypes.

A shortage of feedback is a good illustration of Weak Air supply. It becomes particularly critical when those involved are in a position to exert considerable influence over change. However, as the Centre of Creative Leadership research shows, it does not have to be accepted as inevitable. Conscientious top executives will go out of their way to elicit feedback, to de-emphasize power differences and to get closer in spatial and psychological terms to their employees.

A number of top executives and their organizations have learnt how to generate a Strong Air supply and this is the subject of the next section.

STRONG AIR

For the Air supply in an Ignition type of change to meet the definition of Strong, many elements of the organization have to be pulling in the same direction. We would go so far as to say that the whole corporate culture is involved. Corporate culture, rather like a country's culture, is a mixture of behaviour, attitudes, rewards, patterns of recognition, symbols and rituals. It comes as no surprise therefore to find that a company that provides a Strong Air supply for its new developments does so at many levels.

In Search of Excellence pays homage to 3M's success in providing a Strong Air supply. 3M has a tradition of producing product champions who are the enthusiastic inventors of a new idea or product and who drive the innovation to production and ultimately the market place (sometimes this can be a process lasting several years). The champion is supported in a variety of ways. He or she will have the backing of an executive champion who has been through a similar process and who is there alternatively to push, protect and develop (this role is very similar to the description of 'guides' in the 'Change Really is Change' chapter – see page 55). Not only does the champion receive support from above but also from colleagues and other functions, in the form of a new venture team.

Rather like the teams described in the 'Spark Groups' chapter, the new venture team consists of volunteers drawn from various disciplines and it is granted autonomy. It goes further than a Spark Group, as the assignments to the team are of an indefinite duration. This is undoubtedly costly to 3M, but it is a hallmark of the firm's belief in support that it is prepared to reward successful new developments in monetary terms (in stark contrast to the example quoted earlier under the Weak Air section).

The importance of support or Air, as we call it in the model, cannot be overemphasized. Peters and Waterman sum it up in simple terms: 'Champions are pioneers and pioneers get shot at. The companies that get the most from champions, therefore, are those that have rich support networks so their pioneers will flourish. No support systems, no champions. No champions, no innovations.' The secret appears to be to weave support assumptions into the value system of the culture. Thus 'the would-be champion gains encouragement from the panoply of heroes' tales; don't kill ideas; scrounge; failure is OK.' Over time the values have been institutionalized and it is expected, for example, that scientists will 'bootleg' up to 15 per cent of their time on their own chosen project.

It is the values which give life and 'heart' to any attempt at support on an organizational scale. James Pilditch in *Winning Ways* quotes Christopher Lorenz, management editor of the *Financial Times*, on the subject of 3M. He was asked at a design management conference in London in 1986, why more companies don't learn from 3M and replied, 'Many try to copy 3M. They fail because they adopt the system, but not the culture.'

Having a support system with plenty of Air not only helps companies to develop new products but to handle a host of changes. In the previous section we looked at an example of a promotional system which had far-reaching consequences but which had no real support system, to accompany it. The case study below provides a good counterpoint to that earlier example.

STEPPING DOWN BUT NOT OUT

He was an ebullient, likeable, somewhat over–talkative member of the group. It was with some caution, however, that I approached him at the bar, at the end of the first day of the conference. One of his colleagues had informed me that he had recently been promoted to a management position and then shortly thereafter demoted or 'stepped down' as his company called it, to his former grade.

As I approached, I found him, much to my surprise, holding forth on this very topic. His openness was not just a product of his extrovert nature. He and his colleagues explained that being 'stepped down' carried no stigma in the company and that the whole process was regarded by the top management as a good way of testing a person's capacity for handling new responsibilities. Not only was there the security of a 'soft landing', because the demoted candidate could expect some salary protection, there was also the opportunity for a second bite of the cherry as a person who had been 'stepped down' could re-apply and be accepted for a management job at a later date. The organization, CMG (Computer Management Group UK Services Ltd), an information processing and consulting services company, employs a large proportion of specialists. The move to a management position is a very important one and for most people involved a big change from work based mainly on their specialist skills to significant responsibility for a budget and staff.

In our view, this company has grasped something very important about promotional opportunities. When there is a big step between a person's current job and the first major management position, neither the individual nor the company know how well a promotion is going to work out. There is no better testing ground that a job itself. Temporary failure in this case does not equate with permanent waste. In many organizations we know, this issue is handled badly. Sometimes it is the company that cannot cope. It keeps the individual in the job hoping for improvement, or it moves him sideways into a twilight zone position where it hopes he won't do too much damage. In extremes, it may fire the person. Even if the company can handle demotion, the individual might not be able to, if the move has a lot of stigma attached to it. The attendant feelings of inadequacy may affect current performance and aspirations for the future

Handling Failure

The treatment of failure, whether it is in the promotional arena or in the course of an attempt to tackle something new, is indicative of whether an organization has grasped one of the fundamental aspects of providing support under conditions of change. Change is risky. If an organization wants its employees to take risks, then it must be prepared to accept some mistakes as the cost of risk as well as to enjoy the benefits of successes. One case in point is the treatment of the two individuals who had to carry the responsibility for the failure of the IBM STRETCH computer. 'At the time the program was killed, both the chief designer Stephen Dunwell, and the executive in charge of it, Charlie de Carlo, had gone into the penalty box.' Watson, recalling this, said, 'poor Dunwell had to crawl into a cocoon for three or four years, but I apologised publicly to him later.'

In a similar situation one of our client companies in the finance sector went into a new venture that it knew very little about. Following a series of errors, largely produced by the haste with which the new venture had been pushed by top management, a potential bad debt situation arose. The chief executive had the personal equivalent of a nuclear explosion and blew some of the top management involved out of the organization, while the remainder who were close to the project were effectively 'irradiated' for a long time afterwards. Years later, he decided to express his management style in written form to all his employees and described it as an 'open door' policy. People were encouraged to bring him their problems. A few months elapsed and nobody had walked through his door. He summoned his management team and asked why not a single soul in the entire organization had been to see him. One of the bolder team members took it upon himself to explain, 'You see, Reg, it's because you kill people.'

The idea of putting employees into the equivalent of a state of suspended animation as a result of a mistake is extraordinary. If we take the parallel discussed in the Introduction between human assets and capital assets (see page xv), it is rather like mothballing an expensive piece of equipment because of a temporary defect in one part of its operation. This is particularly bizarre when we consider the rate at which all assets can 'depreciate' under conditions of rapid change. The employee who is left out in the cold for three or more years may be singularly ineffective in keeping pace with the developments happening around him/her.

In writing about the support that organizations need to provide in order to supply the Strong variety of Air we do not intend to imply that it is in some way a soft option. Companies that use it successfully usually demand high standards of performance in return. Dr. Nick Georgiades, while he was Director of Human Resources at British Airways, described the principle as one of 'tough love'. The message that goes out from British Airways is, in effect, 'We the organization will care for you; in return care for the customer and put in a good day's work.' Some 3M champions may be expected to battle on even when the company has not favoured the project with a venture team. The overall atmosphere is sufficiently supportive to encourage the champion to go it alone for a while. It is possible, therefore, to combine the 'softer' aspects of support with the 'harder' aspects of demand for results.

In a revealing study of a Japanese and an American company, Pascale and Athos contrast the culture of the Matsushita Electric company (this includes National and Panasonic) with that of ITT under Geneen's control. Both Matsushita and Geneen were very demanding of employee performance but the main difference in this area was that Geneen combined it with a punishment culture whereas Matsushita favoured praise and positive reinforcement. Interestingly, the two cultures produced very different responses to the problem of the 'failed' executive (discussed above in relation to mistakes and the promotion question). 'When Geneen found an executive wanting, the man was humiliated or fired. When Matsushita made a similar discovery, the man's group was marked as ineffective and he was reassigned, even demoted, and the opportunity for the individual to grow from the experience was stressed.'

In the UK and the US, both of which have cultures in which independence and autonomy are valued, there is nothing sadder that seeing organizations, or individuals, pushed into a set of circumstances where actions are forced upon them. Unfortunately, that phenomenon is all too common in our experience. It usually occurs when people or companies ignore the change messages that surround them. There is an invasive quality about change, as was noted in the Introduction, so ignoring it or even trying to resist it, is usually a fairly short-term enterprise. When it arrives, those who have been denying its very existence are often put in the position of having to take remedial action which they might not otherwise have chosen.

Countless companies have found themselves suddenly having to declare redundancies, spend precious cash on trying to recover shrunken market shares, investigate internal security and discipline or in extreme circumstances, declare bankruptcy. All these actions may be familiar even to organizations with foresight and a proactive approach to change. However, there is a big difference between taking the initiative on tough decisions involving cash or employee numbers and being forced into these decisions without the planning time to determine the best approach. Quite apart from the practical implications, there is a huge psychological gulf between a course of action freely chosen and one imposed by circumstances.

FUEL

It is this distinction between free choice and necessity, between a positive approach to change and a reactive one that we use to define two types of Fuel, Strong and Weak. Organizations operating in a Strong Fuel environment are the ones who are alert to the message of change and in the absence of any new data coming in, actively go out and seek it in the form of specific customer feedback, general market research or analysis of business trends. On the other hand there are organizations operating in a Weak Fuel environment, that is, ignoring or screening out relevant data and certainly not going out and actively seeking customer or competitor information.

WEAK FUEL

It might be argued that if our central thesis is that change is invasive and swift then a proactive approach is not essential. After all, we are not talking about Fuel starvation but a failure to recognize the writing on the wall, the change messages. Messages abound, but the Fuel intake becomes weak when no attention is paid to them. It is remarkable how some companies manage to be so systematically blind. We do not suggest that it is possible for every organization to be at the leading edge of customer and competitor research but rather that they should keep their eyes open for data that is freely available. As Moss Kanter notes, 'Recent business history is filled with the skeletons of companies that failed to innovate or even recognize the need to adapt to obvious change.'

Although information may be freely available it does require a minimum input of energy to assess it. James Pilditch in *Winning Ways* refers to the shock that Sir Peter Parker experienced when as chairman of British Rail he inspected staff lavatories on a railway station. 'He was aghast at the primitive facilities. "Do you expect them to pee in the Boer War?" he asked.' Given that at the time many members of the general public felt that, at a number of stations, they had been 'peeing in the Boer War', it probably would not have come as a shock to them to realize that railway exployees were having to suffer similar facilities.

The radar required to tune into free information may be switched off for a variety of reason. Sometimes it is success itself which causes the problem, as *Business Week* in 1984 noted in an article tracing the downfall of some of the companies such as Levi's, which had been quoted in *In Search of Excellence.* ' "We let the relationship with our retailers fall into a sad state of disrepair", admits one Levi's insider. As the jeans industry grew 15 per cent annually for most of the past 20 years, retailers would sell every pair of jeans that they received from Levi's. That "created tensions in the relationship and unfortunate habits on the part of some of our people", admits President Robert D. Haas, the great-great-grandnephew of founder Levi Strauss. Retailers saw Levi's as aloof and inflexible.'

Any organization confronted by radical change may respond with a reaction of shock. In this respect it is not dissimilar to an individual who may temporarily recoil from a major event because its magnitude has produced an overload of information, stimuli and problems. However, it is what happens next that really determines how healthy the organization is and what its chances of long-term survival are. Our experience is that an organization working in a Weak Fuel environment will either panic or be paralysed.

Panic reactions are easy to detect. They usually become apparent because they bear very little relation to the problem in hand. A classic example would be a sweeping and arbitrary cost-cutting exercise (across the board manpower cuts) or one which is more specific in nature but has savage impact on very small items, (office stationery is a common victim). Most corporate legends have the equivalent of the 'great paperclip purge of '88'.

In the *Under-Insured Insurance Brokers* case study below the reaction following shock was not one of panic but paralysis. Although some companies were prepared for the changes that confronted them, a number were not and their responses ranged from inadequate to non-existent. The surprise is that the signs which heralded the changes were clear and abundant. In other words their Fuel intake was Weak in a Fuel-rich environment.

THE UNDER-INSURED INSURANCE BROKERS

In the early to mid 1980s we worked with a number of UK insurance brokers both large and medium-sized. We have described them as under-insured because their lack of strategic planning, management controls and management development left them very exposed to a variety of risks.

Shrinking capacity in underwriting made it increasingly difficult for brokers to 'place' their business (i.e. find underwriters prepared to underwrite their client risks). Coupled with this, in the words of one broker 'the underwriters weren't giving anything away', that is they were less lenient about ignoring errors and omissions in the agreements with the brokers. There was a time when a certain amount of give and take between broker and underwriter meant that an error or omission on the part of the broker would not necessarily be catastrophic in the event of a claim being made. However, in the changed climate some brokers found themselves holding the baby when it emerged that they had not properly or adequately covered their clients' risks. This was also a time when the stakes on the claims side were getting a good deal higher as time bombs from past activities stopped ticking (the cases of asbestos and Agent Orange herbicide are referred to in the Introduction).

In our work with the brokers, one of the commonest remarks that was made to us, when we started to talk about management development, was that it was unnecessary in what was already essentially a 'people business'. Certainly amongst the Lloyds brokers there was a feeling that the circle of contacts was sufficiently small and reputable for business dealing to be based either on trust built up over the years, or, in the case of a newcomer, a quick face-to-face assessment of their character. A series of scandals shattered the illusion of guaranteed integrity amongst a group of professionals sharing a common interest. The scandals ranged from the minor (accusations of 'sharp practice') through the probably criminal (tax evasion schemes) to the major crimes of misappropriation of funds. To an outsider, news of these scandals was not entirely unexpected because the second most common comment we heard (after 'broking is a people business') was that 'brokers are opportunists'. In an atmosphere of opportunism and very few management controls it follows that some people are going to be tempted to break the rules.

Opportunism was the defence that was quoted to us by those in the industry who had a natural loathing of strategic planning. In some ways this can be an attractive philosophy as long as it doesn't lead to the acquisition of unprofitable business and an overall lack of direction. The lack of direction of some of the medium-sized brokers left them as sitting targets for some of the really big players in the market who were hungry for making takeover bids or who wanted to add a different type of business to an existing financial conglomerate.

All the problems outlined above were capable of remedy but all too often we witnessed responses that were unproductive or negative. The errors and omissions problem was 'covered' by additional provision in the balance sheet but the problem was not really tackled at source. If it was tackled at source rather than the symptom level it was through the vehicle of training manuals for junior staff. Rarely did we see this training stemming from a philosophy which would have placed some of the responsibility on the management's shoulders. Perhaps that was not surprising because the terms 'management' and 'management development' had negative connotations (they were synonymous with 'discipline' to some people) and were very much under-valued compared with the excitement of being a broker.

Case Study

Better management practices might also have gone some way towards preventing some of the scandals. We were keen to help our clients to place their assessment of others on a more rational footing and to leave less to chance. Traditional management approaches in the planning areas would certainly have helped one client that seemed determined to leave itself as the victim of circumstance, hoping that something good would come along before the inevitable hostile takeover bid.

End Case Study

The case study illustrates the consequences of operating in a Weak Fuel environment and ignoring the importance of detecting and responding to signs which indicate that a change is needed. As we have said earlier however, although the initial reaction to major new events might often be shock, this does not have to mean that the ensuing response is a negative one. Organizations that have a degree of preparedness of both a physical variety (budget, resources, training) and a psychological variety (anticipation, new attitudes) can produce a positive response. The following section on Strong Fuel looks in detail at the elements of a positive response.

STRONG FUEL

An organization operating in a Weak Fuel environment has been defined as failing to realize the significance of and failing to react to, abundant mesages about change. In contrast, therefore, the organization operating in a Strong Fuel situation can be defined as one which is highly responsive to messages about change. In the absence of fresh data it actively seeks information about the outside environment, with the aim of feeding that information into its decision-making processes. Japanese companies are renowned for being aware of what the competition is doing and turning it to their advantage. Observers have attributed this to the influence of the Samurai philosophy, which stresses the importance of the warrior being able to place himself, psychologically, in the shoes of the enemy. Japan Air Lines, for example, are sufficiently interested in the competition to have a team of full-time staff travelling with and surveying the other airlines.

Some organizations, which take the innovation and development process seriously, also encourage the active search for ideas that are genuinely novel and are born out of creative thinking processes, rather than out of existing information. There are, therefore, three ways of getting into a Strong Fuel position. The approach which requires the least commitment of time and resources is sensitivity to freely available information. Hunting for information which is not readily available is harder work. The third approach, of creatively generating ideas out of a void, is the most demanding approach of all.

Sensitivity to Freely Available Information

Some information about organizations is so readily available that it is hard to avoid. In the case of a large corporation, public or private, large cross-sections of the community will fall into one of the categories of customer, supplier, shareholder or competitor.

There can be nothing more demoralizing than being an employee, particularly one with significant decision-making responsibilities, whose employer has a poor public reputation. During a period of Rolls Royce's history it had become a standing joke, amongst some sections of the community in Derby, that a proportion of the shop-floor workforce favoured a regular day's sick leave in the mid-week period to prepare for the working Sunday on double pay. Sometimes the joke becomes very public indeed and there have been times in British Leyland's history when a jibe at its strike record or demarcation disputes has become part of the cabaret act of stand-up comedians. During our employment with a major building society, in a relatively successful phase of its development, we found that even a visit to our local squash club would invite a host of comments from other members who were having difficulties with their local branch or who had been refused a mortgage.

As was noted in the section about Weak Fuel, one of the key factors in a company's success is the ability to be alert to free information and then act on it. Some Chief Executives and Presidents are so hungry to know what their customers think that they make sure that they know first hand what is happening. *In Search of Excellence* refers to Jo Willard Marriott Senior, of Marriott Hotels group, who 'until recently . . . read every customer complaint card.' Rocco Forte, Chief Executive of The Forte Group, 'sees all complaints that come to company headquarters and follows them up personally with the head of the division concerned. If the complaint is serious, he insists on seeing the report of the investigation and what has been done to satisfy the customer.'

Sir Colin Marshall is reputed to have taken a similar approach when he took over as Chief Executive of British Airways. This seems to have been motivated by the realization that the messages he was getting about passenger satisfaction from within the organization did not match up with the poorer reputation he must already have been aware of, via the media and his own experience.

Sensitivity to the data is not, by itself, enough. The organization then has to take strategic and tactical decisions to act on it. In the case of British Leyland, Michael Edwardes recognized the link that existed not only between quality and customer satisfaction but between quality and employee morale. 'It is very difficult to put one's heart and soul into the manufacture of something that has become a standing joke. Jaguar owners in the United States were supposed to have two vehicles: one for driving and the other to cannibalize for spare parts when the first broke down. So Edwardes made the launch of the first new car under the new management an exercise in employee morale building by hammering away to convince them its quality would be equal to or better than anything produced by competitors . . . He talks of a "commitment to perfection" which engendered a sense of excitement and caused previously demoralized employees to work exceptionally long hours.' The significance of this example is Edwardes' recognition that it mattered what the public said about Leyland cars, not just because that was a barometer of how many they would buy but because his own employees needed to be associated with a product synonymous with quality and achievement.

Hunting for Information

It may be the case that there is not enough free information to put an organization in a Strong Fuel position. The organization may not be big enough to attract the widespread attention associated with the examples given above, or its products or services may not be as visible and as widely discussed as a car, for example. If an organization is serious about wanting to be in a Strong Fuel position it may, therefore, have to expend some time and money. In the case of Sainsbury this is a major commitment. Goldsmith and Clutterbuck quote Sir John Sainsbury as saying 'we are unusual in the retail world in the importance we have always attached to (market research). Data concerning the general marketplace in terms of the nation's economy, food trends and socio-economic environment are constantly updated and analysed . . . Competitors' developments in terms of new stores, marketing strategies and prices are examined closely.'

A company such as Sainsbury clearly has the resources to put behind the kind of market research approach described above (although it could be argued that it is because of their market research approach that they are successful enough to fund expensive research). Actively hunting for information does not have to be such an expensive venture. Peters recalls a young man who kept pestering him, following a detailed talk about surveying customer satisfaction, to provide him with the 'answer'. 'Frustrated I thought for a moment, then blurted out "Look, just drag fifteen customers in here from somewhere, buy 'em lunch or dinner and ask them what the heck is on their minds".'

Surveying customer opinion is not just a neutral activity in the way that a thermometer will measure room temperature without affecting what it is supposed to be measuring. The method of hunting for information should ideally be seen in a positive light by those being canvassed. After all, they will be giving up time to respond to an interviewer or to fill in a questionnaire. One of the simplest means of encouraging customers to take part in surveys is to make it clear that the information gained will be read or listened to and acted on. Ideally some of the survey information should be responded to, such as when a customer has taken the time and trouble to provide detailed comment or write a letter. Having had a mainly enjoyable stay, although with rather mixed service, in a hotel in the Middle East which is part of an international chain, we took the trouble to fill out a lengthy guest feedback form. We were greatly impressed when a letter was sent to our UK address some weeks later, responding to some of the specific comments that we had made. More impressive still was the fact that they remembered what we had said when we revisited them a year later.

Ideas out of a Void

Sometimes an organization wants to go beyond what is obtainable for free or from some market research. It may want to lead a market trend, rather than follow one. Starting with a blank sheet of paper and filling it with ideas can be a very tough and demanding approach. Having been part of a successful experiment at Ashridge Management College to do just that, we can vouch for its difficulty. We needed to create a management training programme on the subject of teamworking that was genuinely new and different, if it was to make its way in a marketplace full of teamworking ideas and models, some of them very old indeed. We decided to take the approach of emptying our minds of the theories and models that we already knew, to substitute a new and usable vocabulary and rely heavily on the raw data produced by our own experience with our client companies. The most difficult thing of all was the attempt to wipe the slate clean by pretending we had forgotten our previous academic training.

Perhaps the blank sheet of paper approach is the most radical and demanding of all. Professor Michael Kirton distinguishes between the type of personality capable of innovating and the type who prefes to adapt. Innovators are able to see beyond the rules and boundaries of a problem and can adopt a 'do it differently' approach. They are also likely to proliferate their ideas. Adaptors, on the other hand have a more incremental, 'do it better approach' of progressively modifying what is already there. They are likely to produce a sufficiency of ideas and stop when they think that they've got a good one. The interesting thing about both types is that they are capable of generating new ideas.

If the 'innovators' as described above are in short supply in the organization then there are two possible responses. One is to encourage the ones that do exist, giving them the Strong Air that they need in order to be able to breathe. The other is to encourage the adaptors in their efforts. Although they may not be producing new ideas literally out of a void, they may still be producing creative solutions. Naisbitt and Aburdene quote the example of an employee of a Swedish pulp and paper mill, building a greenhouse for the production of 125 tons per annum of commercial grade tomatoes, using the excess heat from the mill. In an interesting contrast, usable stocks of coal stood in frozen heaps throughout the British miners' strike in the mid 1970s while nearby cooling towers poured the heat from the power stations into the air.

Case Study

THE SHOW WITH EVERYTHING

In our own consulting experience, British Airways stands out as a good example of an organization that over recent years has got itself into a Strong Fuel position. It has done this in a variety of ways but a cornerstone even from the start of the revolution ushered in by Sir Colin Marshall has been a continuous Customer First initiative, stressing the importance to the business of the customer. Part of this initiative has been a series of corporate training programmes which have developed a number of themes including an emphasis on interpersonal skills, the importance of co-operative teamwork and an awareness of the different component parts of the organization. The 1987/88 corporate programme was the most ambitious to date

and was perhaps only possible becaue of the predecessor programmes on whose shoulders it stood. Titled 'To Be The Best' it was an
attempt to enhance competitor awareness across the whole
organization and to encourage the various departments within B.A.
to gear themselves to meet the competitive challenge. We regard it
as a good example of putting the principles of Strong Fuel into
practice in a training context.

The 1987/88 Customer First initiative which had 'To Be The
Best' as part of it, also included a novel way of finding out about
passenger opinion. Any passengers arriving off a B.A. flight in
Terminal 4 of Heathrow Airport could, if they so wished,
immediately record their impressions of the service they had just
received. By stepping into a small booth with a video camera
recording facility they were guaranteed that their views would be
heard and seen by British Airways staff. Where the comments related
to a particular flight, the crew were shown the video. From month
to month a cross–section of videos, bringing both good and bad
news, were replayed to an audience in excess of 100 at the 'To Be
The Best' programme. A member of B.A. Catering might see, in
Technicolor and appearing on 16 video screens simultaneously a
customer full of praise for one of the meals or expressing heartfelt
disgust at a sticky offering served up on one of the flights. Thus the
hunting for information approach, advocated above, gives results in
a very tangible and public way.

The 'To Be The Best' programme not only celebrated the
importance of information hunting, it also took full advantage of
free information. At least an hour of the day was devoted to sharing
facts and figures about the competition, presented in an attractive
and illuminating fashion. Perhaps the most important source of free
information was that provided by the participants themselves. Many
had valuable experience of the airline and its competition and were

encouraged to express their views in open debate and discussion during the day.

As well as making liberal use of information hunting and free information, the 'To Be The Best' programme also had its fair share of opportunities for ideas generation. Participants were encouraged to create, discover and discuss ways of improving their own functional areas in order to beat the competition. The best of the ideas were relayed back to the appropriate member of management for action.

As with anything as ambitious as this programme, it had its problems. In an organization as large as B.A. there are always some cynics who see any management initiative as manipulation. Also, on a mixed programme, what is a highbrow idea for one person may be a lowbrow idea for another. Nevertheless, it is still an excellent vehicle for generating Strong Fuel, by putting a large number of individuals in touch with good quality information about the outside environment, encouraging them to discuss its implications and inviting them to generate some of their own ideas.

End Case Study

Strong Fuel/Strong Medicine

A Strong Fuel environment can be a tough one in which to operate. Feedback from the outside world may not be positive and if it really is accepted in its raw form, without any editing or attempt to package it, then it arrives in the organization without any respect of internal politics or sensitivities. We noted in the introduction how change had a habit of being invasive and quoted the example of the Challenger disaster. Because of the public nature of that disaster, NASA had to face the consequences of its errors immediately and in a very painful way. The ripples from that episode have not yet subsided.

We also noted that there is a randomness to change and this too serves to make the Strong Fuel environment quite a hard one with which to work. Some of the news coming into the organization will be a complete surprise. One major airline was informed by a firm of specialist advisers on future trends that one of its most dangerous competitors in the future would probably be a currently non-existent competitor that would grow rapidly from nowhere and establish a foothold in a specialist corner of the market.

Although the environment that we are describing can be a tough one it can also be very rewarding. People who are accustomed to working in such an environment are able to turn the surprise of new information into optimism and excitement. This is in marked contrast to the Weak Fuel environment, described earlier, where a common reaction to surprise is panic. In the example quoted above of the airline threatened by the spectre of a non-existent competitor, an assertive response on the part of the airline would be to make its own surprise entry into a new market.

We were fascinated to observe that the presenters who ran the 'To Be The Best' event applied their own principles to themselves in a very honest and open way. One of them, who was relatively new to the job of addressing an audience of 100 or more, was keen to know how he had performed after the first pilot run of the programme. It had been a long and gruelling day, and there had been various technical difficulties. His own performance had been competent but lacked the sparkle and polish needed to lift the programme. We winced as he approached members of the audience who had been very patient throughout the day but who had not had the benefit of the smooth production that would eventually become the hallmark of the finished programme. They were polite but frank with him and we feared the potentially demoralizing effect that their feedback would be having. But far from being downhearted, he appeared to be re-energized by his audience's comments and eager for the following day when he could try out a number of improvements.

The conclusion, therefore, is that a Strong Fuel environment may be tough but it doesn't have to be miserable. The shock that may accompany new information does not have to lead to panic. In

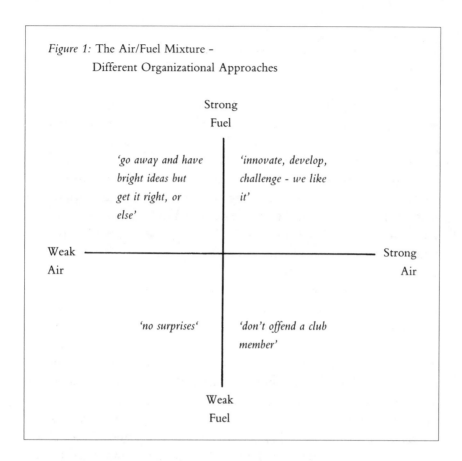

Figure 1: The Air/Fuel Mixture –
Different Organizational Approaches

Strong
Fuel

'go away and have bright ideas but get it right, or else'

'innovate, develop, challenge - we like it'

Weak
Air

Strong
Air

'no surprises'

'don't offend a club member'

Weak
Fuel

the right setting, with people who are not afraid of change, it can lead to effective action.

THE MIXTURE

Given that both Fuel and Air can come in Strong and Weak varieties, this suggests four possible combinations; Strong Fuel/Strong Air, Weak Fuel/Strong Air, Weak Fuel/Weak Air, Strong Fuel/Weak Air. In our work we have come to recognize certain sorts of organizational culture that are associated with these four combinations, and they are identified in Fig. 1 and in the following descriptions.

Strong Fuel/Strong Air

This is without doubt the most exciting and challenging work environment. What the organization is saying to its employees is 'innovate, develop, challenge - we like it.' There is a readiness to face up to information about the business from both within and without, whether it is good news or bad. If the information is not readily to hand then people are encouraged to go and seek it out. For those individuals who are able to act on the information that they have found and for those who can innovate, there is plenty of encouragement. The encouragement has an emotional component, that is, spoken praise and support when conditions are stressful, and also a more tangible component such as pay rises or promotions for pioneering work.

Weak Fuel/Strong Air

This is a rather unusual environment, for it could be argued that in the absence of good quality information or innovative ideas there is not much to support and encourage. What seems to be happening in this kind of organization is that people experience the environment as warm and supportive until they attempt to do something out of the ordinary. It is as if the organization is saying 'don't offend a club member.' Some of the public sector organizations in which we worked during the mid 1970s had this kind of atmosphere. There was employment security, slow but steady pay and promotional rises and often a good social life outside work. However, there was a selective deafness when it came to listening to critical comments from outside, and the employees who were truly innovative often found themselves losing heart in the face of the rule book or layers of bureaucratic decision-making.

Weak Fuel/Weak Air

Perhaps this organization is best characterized by the well known quote from Geneen, who at one time was head of ITT, when he said that large corporations wanted 'no surprises'. It also appears that Geneen ran ITT with tight controls and measures with a lot of cross-checking and very little support or encouragement. The 'no surprises' atmosphere must have been stifling to innovation and coupled with the absence of support this suggests a Weak Fuel/Weak Air environment.

By rights, the Weak Fuel/Weak Air organization should not survive in the long term. In the 90s with the forces of change as described in the Introduction, it seems inconceivable that a 'no surprises' culture could exist. Indeed one would suspect that for this type of company the biggest surprise of all – plummeting performance figures – could be just around the corner.

However, there do seem to be companies that can survive with a Weak Fuel/Weak Air mixture; they are very often chasing short-term profitability in an atmosphere of strict financial controls. If they do survive it is usually because an individual or group of individuals at the centre is providing the Fuel. This puts a lot of onus on that individual or group and begs several questions about succession when they depart. This is exactly what is reputed to have happened in the case of Geneen and ITT. Pascale and Athos report Geneen's failure to handle succession adequately and they quote one top manager as having said 'He was like de Gaulle - no one could replace him but someone had to succeed him.'

Even if a Weak Fuel/Weak Air organization is surviving, it seems unlikely to be stable in the long term. Once whoever is holding it together at the centre departs the organization must either evolve rapidly to compensate for the deficit in both areas or it will suffer.

Strong Fuel/Weak Air

This is probably the most high-risk environment of all the four types for the average employee. There is simultaneously an atmosphere which encourages responsiveness to the outside and the generation of new ideas, but very little support and encouragement. The message from the organization is either implicitly or explicitly, 'go away and have bright ideas but get it right, or else.'

During the early 1980s mortgage funds went from famine to feast in a very short space of time. One of our clients, a building society, took very firm action during the famine. It let it be known that all its branch managers were expected to stay within the centrally prescribed guidelines for lending or face the first stage of the disciplinary procedure. These guidelines effectively restricted lending to young married couples who were first time buyers and established investors with the society. Once the mortgage funds surplus began to emerge and the banks started to compete with the building societies in offering mortgages, our client sent out a directive encouraging managers actively to seek opportunities for lending. Far from being stimulated by this invitation to lend creatively, most managers stuck very closely to the old guidelines. They had become so used to erring on the side of conservatism that they were too timid to step into the brave new world which was being offered to them.

There are some individuals and some organizations that can manage to innovate in a risky, unsupportive environment. However, this requires energy and courage and once these run out the Strong Air/Weak Air situation will tend towards Weak Fuel/ Weak Air.

THE RIGHT MIXTURE FOR IGNITION

There is no doubt that an atmosphere of Strong Fuel/Strong Air is most likely to help the kind of swift change being discussed in this book. Although it is an atmosphere which is difficult to attain, once it has been achieved it is, to an extent, self-sustaining. People with ideas who are given encouragement to discuss them and act on them are likely to generate more ideas. The more they enjoy their success, the greater their morale is likely to be and the greater the chance that they will feel positively towards their colleagues and give them support and encouragement.

Translating an idea into action, especially if it involves a change in the established way of doing things, can require special qualities. It is these special qualities that are considered in the next section on Sparks. The Spark is the final element that transforms the Air/Fuel Mixture into Ignition.

AIR FUEL MIXTURE

Air Can be defined as the different forms of atmosphere in which change takes place.

Fuel Can be defined as the ideas and stimuli which drive the change forward.

Air

- As a minimum, key people involved in any change effort need some of the barriers and obstacles to their ideas and actions to be removed.

- Air can be Weak or Strong

- When the Air is Weak, the organization's message is, 'Fine, we won't stop you, but you realize this will have to be done in your own time'. A supportive atmosphere is missing. A shortage of feedback is often an indication of the presence of Weak Air in an organization.

- When the Air is Strong, the organization's message is, 'We the organization will care for you; in return, care for the customer and put in a good day's work'. The atmosphere is supportive, but the demand for results remains high. Often, if Air is Strong in an organization, the whole corporate culture is involved in the change and many elements of the organization are pulling in the same direction.

Fuel

- There can be a positive approach to change or a reactive approach.

- Fuel can be Weak or Strong.

- When the Fuel is Weak, people in the organization fail to realize the significance of and fail to react to the messages about change. They often ignore or screen out relevant data and certainly don't go out and actively seek customer or competitor information. Weak Fuel can often be recognized when the organization is in a state of panic or is paralysed.

- When the Fuel is Strong, people in organizations are highly responsive to messages about change. In the absence of fresh data, the organization actively seeks information about the outside environment, with the aim of feeding that information into its decision-making processes.

THE MIXTURE

The Air/Fuel mixture can take four different forms:

- *Strong Fuel/Strong Air:* here the organizational stance is: 'Innovate, develop, challenge – we like it.'

- *Weak Fuel/Strong Air:* here the organizational stance is: 'Don't offend a club member'. People experience the environment as warm and supportive, until they try to do something out of the ordinary.

- *Weak Fuel/Weak Air:* here the organizational stance is: 'No surprises'. The atmosphere is not supportive and relevant data is often not generated.

- *Strong Fuel/Weak Air:* here the organizational stance is: 'Go away and have bright ideas but get it right or else . . .'. There is an atmosphere which encourages responsiveness to the outside and the generation of new ideas but at the same time there is very little support and encouragement.

IGNITION

An atmosphere of *Strong Fuel/Strong Air* is most likely to help the kind of swift change that Ignition is made of.

REFERENCES

- Naisbitt, J. and Aburdene, P. (1985) *Re-inventing the Corporation,* New York: Warner Books.

- Moss Kanter, R. *Power Failure in Management Circuits,* Harvard Business Review July–August 1979.

- Kaplan, R.E., Drath, W.M. and Kofodimos, J.R. *Power and Getting Criticism,* Issues and Observations (Centre for Creative Leadership, U.S.A) Vol 4, No 3 August 1984.

- Peters, T.J. and Waterman, R.H. (1982) *In Search of Excellence,* New York: Harper and Row.

- Pilditch, J. (1987) *Winning Ways,* New York: Harper and Row.

- Fishman, K.D. (1981) *The Computer Establishment* New York: Harper and Row.

- Moss Kanter, R. (1985) *The Change Masters,* London: Unwin Paperbacks.

- *Who's Excellent Now?* Business Week November 1984.

- Hodgson, G. (1984) *Lloyds of London: A Reputation at Risk,* Harmondsworth: Penguin Books.

- Goldsmith, W. and Clutterbuck, D. (1984) *The Winning Streak,* London: Weidenfeld and Nicolson

- Peters, T.J. (1987) *Thriving on Chaos,* New York: Knopf.

- McHale, J. and Flegg, D. *Innovators rule OK – or do they?* Training and Development October 1986.

- Kirton, M.J. *Adaptors and Innovators: A Description and Measure,* Journal of Applied Psychology 1976.

Section II

Generating Sparks

2. Change Really is Change

'King or beggar, everything is brief and changing'
(attributed to Sheikh Zayed bin Sultan al Nahyan, President of the United Arab Emirates)

The individual that we have come to label as a Spark is the person who has grasped the message that 'Change Really is Change'. This is the individual who seems to thrive on the altered circumstances and on the fluidity of the situation. It is the person who is not secretly waiting for things to return to the status quo or fighting his or her own personal rearguard action. We have identified a number of elements which contribute to this readiness to change:

1. *Looking for the signposts:* this is the skill of using freely available information about people, places and businesses in order to develop a reliable understanding of a new situation.

2. *Expecting signposts to move:* in a truly fluid situation, the fact that a signpost says one thing one day does not mean it will say the same thing on another occasion.

3. *Looking for guides (in unexpected places):* there may well be people on hand who can help to provide some of the cues and clues in a changing situation, but in an organizational setting, they may not be the people traditionally associated with giving advice.

4. *Questioning every assumption:* if 'Change Really is Change' then there is very little that has to remain static or fixed, which means that all assumptions are potentially open to question (later in the chapter we look at the few important things that are worth keeping fixed).

5. *Not settling down too quickly:* change, of the variety we describe in the Introduction, has a habit of not having a chance to stabilize before it is nudged out of the way by the next development coming behind it and so it pays both individuals and organizations not to settle down too quickly.

In order to illustrate the elements of readiness to change, we have chosen as a case study the experience of a group of managers in a Middle East oil company. These managers were being developed for senior positions in the organization. Part of their development included an intensive management training programme run by Mara Consultants and a group of colleagues from Ashridge Management College. The case is particularly appropriate because it highlights change at the micro level of the individual, through to the macro level of the company and ultimately the country's economy.

The setting in the Middle East country of Jebel Arabia is significant. While no country named Jebel Arabia actually exists, its ingredients are all realistic. Like many of its neighbours, Jebel Arabia is at one and the same time rooted in the conservative traditions of Islam and undergoing the immense upheaval of rapid economic growth that has been taking place since the 1960s. Even the towns that previously existed as ports, consist of 80 per cent of new buildings, erected over the last 20 years. Permanence and impermanence exist side by side. The Arab adheres to the historical principles of Islam and at the same time treats everything in business as negotiable, changeable and ultimately open to the will of Allah. The image of shifting sands is hard to avoid. In a literal sense, sand continually encroaches on the towns as if to serve as a reminder of where they have come from.

```
Case Study
```

SHIFTING SANDS

Background

The company in question, Jebel Arabia National Oil (JANO) is involved in the exploration, refining and distribution of its country's most precious natural asset. Like those of many Middle East countries, the fortunes of Jebel Arabia's economy are very closely related to the health of its oil company. Most of the new building, foreign investment and service industries have only been made possible as a result of the spectacular oil revenues of the 1970s.

It might be argued that both JANO and the country have already seen the most significant changes that they are likely to face in the form of a huge social, political and economic upheavals that accompany a sudden influx of wealth. Along with the influx of wealth came an influx of expatriate labour and indeed much of JANO's success would not have been possible without substantial investment from foreign oil companies, both in money and people terms. Specialists and managers from the western countries have had a major influence in shaping JANO's destiny. Lower down the labour market, both in the oil company and elsewhere, there is a high proportion of Indian and Pakistani workers. In the mid to late 1980s, however, both the oil company and the country were facing some important developments. The effects of the vast oil revenues from earlier years were still being felt, but at the same time the future looked less assured (oil prices went down to less than US$10 a barrel, in 1986, for example). A walk around the main city suggested growth but the talk in the boardrooms was of caution. In order to build its economic and cultural future on a firmer footing, JANO decided to attempt to reduce its reliance on foreign expertise by promoting local Arab nationals into key management and specialist positions within the company. The term 'local' here distinguishes the Jebel Arabians from the Arabs from neighbouring countries. This latter group, being relatively small in number, was not radically affected, unlike the other foreign nationals who had traditionally held a high proportion of important jobs.

At one level there was an attempt to alter the corporate culture to protect and develop the more talented members of the local populace, but because the oil company was so important to Jebel Arabia, it was also an attempt to re-assert a number of cultural and religious values. Central to this were the individuals involved who had to undergo a personal cultural change to learn the techniques of running a large corporation. Finally there was my own role as external consultant, briefed with providing management training to help the process along. I was at one and the same time peripheral to the main changes that were happening yet very much involved at the level of new learning (both the participants' and my own).

In the course of training a cross-section of aspiring senior managers I came across a wide range of preparedness for change and it was instructive to identify those individuals who would grasp the opportunity that was given to them (the Sparks, in our analysis). At the same time I had to cope with my own challenges as I attempted to operate in an unfamiliar culture. Very often the two situations paralleled each other and led me to some general conclusions about trying to master the principle of 'change really is change'.

The Change Challenge

The enormity of the task facing the group that JANO has chosen to promote and to develop with intensive management education, should not be underestimated. Many of them were only one generation away from a group of people that had made their living by pearl-diving, fishing and trading. A number of them hung on to small trading businesses that they attempted to run in parallel with their principal job with JANO. At a personal level they had to make the transition from thinking instinctively as traders to the more regimented demands of management in a large bureaucracy.

However, there was a second transition which will be explored in the section of the case study about Releasing Creativity. JANO needed people who could not only manage but who could also think. Any country dependent on a resource (in this case hydrocarbons) that is both prone to world price fluctuations and ultimately exhaustible in supply has to find a new way of building future economic security.

The Group of Managers

JANO had hand picked about 20 middle managers for the two week development course that I was to run. Interestingly the group contained a cross-section of backgrounds, and although the majority were local Arab nationals there was a handful of other nationalities represented there too. This signalled an important aspect of the thinking of all those who were involved with the 'Arabization' programme: that there was still a lot to be learnt from expatriates and although they might be blocked from some key jobs, it would still be vital to have co-operation between the different national and racial groups in the company.

The typical participant was not really cosmopolitan in outlook. Most were, by and large, adhering to the principles laid down by Islam and leading fairly ordered and controlled lives. Many of them, however, had been educated overseas in the UK or USA and exposed to different cultures and ways of living. The individuals who appeared to be the most likely ones to handle the change that would face them in their new roles within JANO – the Sparks in our analysis – were the ones who had learnt and benefited from their overseas experience. This does not mean that they swallowed a foreign culture hook line and sinker, but that they were alert to the features of the overseas environment and had the ability to interact comfortably with it. In business terms this meant that they understood some of the American management theory and the lessons to be learnt from the US corporates. They were also interested in the similarities and differences of the American and the Japanese approaches to questions of leadership and strategy.

In a phrase used earlier in this chapter, they were able to 'look for the signposts' in a new environment. That is, they could rapidly sum up a new situation by picking up on the readily available cues and clues about behaviour, norms and customs. There were times when this had rather amusing consequences. In the course of one mealtime I might be engaged in conversation about a Hydrocracker Project, the Iran/Iraq conflict and the joys of the time some of the participants had spent in the leafy London suburb of Putney. However, the important benefit to them was that they could apply the same technique of 'looking for the signposts' in the foreign environment of complex management problems.

From my own point of view, signpost watching was of the utmost importance. It took me some time to realize, in the early days of my contacts with JANO senior managers to set up the training, that the lengthy greetings and the tea drinking at every meeting, were important rituals. At the same time I had to maintain my own values about not being deflected from my purpose. Given that I was being hired to disseminate best practice in the areas of planning and decision making, I needed to be firm about getting agreements about schedules and deadlines.

The Managers' Expectations

It is one thing to have the ability to look out for and read a signpost which carries information about a country's culture or a management culture, but quite another skill to be able to anticipate that the signposts might move, point in a new direction or carry a different message. This is one of the skills of change preparedness, and we see it as very much part of the repertoire of the Spark who is at the centre of change initiatives. In terms of their expectations of the future, the participants could be divided into three broad categories. There were those who simply took the present economy together with their own lifestyle and extrapolated it into the future. This could be described as the 'business as usual' outlook, resting on the assumption that the parks kept green by highly expensive de-salinated water and the air-conditioned Mercedes would automatically be around for ever. If this group could be described as wildly optimistic, then the second group was equally blinkered in its pessimism. Its basic view of life was that everything would revert to desert and that future generations might well have to return to the Bedouin existence.

The group that was really exciting, in terms of its outlook, was composed of people who realized that the conditions under which JANO was operating were changing radically and that a future of green parks and high standards of living was possible only if new products were developed and new markets discovered. They believed that they could avoid re-joining their ancestors in the desert, but only through a concerted effort and innovative action. For example, they recognized the limitations of an economy massively dependent on hydrocarbon products. They could see that the signposts were going to shift and were ready to read them.

This group, the Sparks, as I came to think of them, differed from the pessimists in other ways. Even at the height of the conflict between neighbouring Iran and Iraq, in 1987, they did not assume that the war would go on for decades. Subsequent events bore them out. They could not be certain, of course, which way the conflict would go but they were not hooked into thinking that because it had already lasted a long time, this had to be the pattern for evermore.

Interestingly, they also differed from the optimists in certain important respects. All three groups had invested in equities but it was only the optimists who had failed to grasp the principle that values can fall as well as rise. During my time with them, we had to devote a large section of a finance tutorial explaining to the optimists what had happened to their personal wealth following a dip in the world stock market. The Sparks weren't pleased about the turn of events but had enough flexibility not to be thrown off course by the news.

Another distinguishing feature of the Sparks was their response to learning. The course had been designed along a popular western principle of management education that people learn best by discovering things themselves through activity and participation. I was warned that this principle might not translate well into a culture that viewed education as something taught to novices by experts. Certainly it was necessary to do more 'teaching' than would be comfortable with a British or American audience, but the really heartening aspect of the experience with JANO was that the self-directed discovery approach to learning started to pay dividends as the course progressed. Noticeably, the first group to take to it were the Sparks who were able to put any discomfort to one side and see the value in the approach.

My own parallel experience of shifting signposts revolved around the thorny problem of who my true client was. Protocol dictated that my early contact was very high up the organization, but although this senior manager had the ultimate cheque-signing authority, he was heavily reliant on the advice of his personnel specialists. Despite his need for advice, he was quite capable of

Case Study

ignoring their views altogether and making a completely different decision of his own. Most of the time he negotiated with me through his subordinates but there were occasions, even during the later stages of the project when he wanted to deal with me direct.

Making the whole situation more complex was the fact that the personnel specialists did not present a united front. There was a likeable inexperienced local, Rafiq, learning the trade from an experienced Dutchman, Jan. The third character was a wily Jordanian, Jawad, who had the ear of the senior manager. He knew that, under the new scheme of promoting local nationals, Rafiq would one day take his job, but did not want to do anything to hasten the event, without appearing to be actively obstructive. Jan was excluded from the power struggle by virtue of his nationality but had more technical expertise than the other two combined.

In dealing with the specialists and their senior manager, I could not escape the metaphor of shifting sands. The relationships were constantly changing, making the process of establishing agreements very difficult indeed. My only salvation was to take my own advice about moving signposts and to anticipate that agreements would be altered, revised and re-negotiated at the whim of any one of the four people involved.

Getting Help

The aspiring senior managers on the training course were faced with a very daunting task. Not only did they have to tackle the problems outlined earlier in the case study, *(The Change Challenge)* they had to prepare themselves for a considerable amount of isolation. Once promoted, they would be in the unenviable position of managing foreign nationals who not only possessed much expertise but who under normal circumstances would also have expected to be occupying the senior jobs.

This raised the interesting question of where the up and coming managers should go to get advice and guidance. The more alert and aware managers (the Sparks) recognized the problem, unlike some of their colleagues who were clearly going to attempt to muddle through and would sometimes be forced to re-discover some of the knowledge and experience that was already in the company. Although they were few in number, there were some local nationals who had done well in the organization prior to the accelerated promotion scheme. Some of the Sparks had been able to identify established individuals who might help them in their own careers.

Perhaps the most interesting route was taken by the managers who had identified some trusted foreign nationals who could be relied upon to provide sound advice, even though their own prospects of promotion were severely limited. To take the earlier example of the personnel specialists, Rafiq would have been naive to treat Jawad as a guide and mentor but Jan proved to be very helpful and assisted Rafiq on a number of occasions.

Operating as I was, several thousand miles away from home, I too felt the need for guides on occasion. Both Jan and Rafiq filled these roles in their different ways, Rafiq giving useful insights into the Jebel Arabia culture. Perhaps the most unexpected guidance came from a highly opinionated course participant who at first seemed to be putting all his energies into manoeuvering me into complex arguments. Having put me through this testing phase, he then decided that I had been tormented enough and proceeded to share a wealth of insights and anecdotes which were a considerable help to me in avoiding cultural gaffes during the course.

Releasing Creativity
In an earlier chapter, The Air/Fuel Mixture, (see pages 3–34) the distinction was drawn between people who amend a situation or

product by incremental degrees (the adaptors) and those who go for radical revision (the innovators). Both types were present in the group of managers that I was training and both in their own ways were displaying Spark behaviour.

The Spark needed to carry JANO forward was recognition that a reliance on the simple extraction and export of crude oil was a very limiting strategy. Clearly JANO's future lay with the development of its 'downstream' business (that is, diversification into a host of refined products). JANO had, in fact, already taken some steps in this direction. The innovators in the group were excited by the prospect of developments in the areas of gas and fertilizer, and the more far-sighted individuals could see the possibility of downstream investment in other countries' refineries.

Although the adaptors were clearly more conservative in their outlook, and tended to stay with problems more closely related to crude oil extraction, they too had a contribution to make to the creativity debate. For example, they grasped the importance of not following the route of some middle eastern producers who were trying to maximize output. They realized that an approach that was different from the one adopted by their neighbours was called for, and they favoured instead strategies of conservation to sustain the source of wealth in the long term. Many of them were also interested in the use of sophisticated seismic exploration techniques to find new reserves.

Part of my job as the tutor of the management training programme was to persuade them to use the creativity (either adaptive or innovative) of which they were capable. Much of their previous training as engineers concentrated on what was certain, measurable, sensible and practical. They took some persuading that the world of management and especially the world of creative management, could be ill-defined, ambiguous and full of possibilities, imagination and novelty. Although previous conditioning can be an immense stumbling-block to any new learning, with the willing commitment of the learner it is possible to break new ground and this was certainly true of some of the JANO managers.

One of the exercises on the training course, which gave some clues as to the participant's creativity, involved a group discussion about a survival situation and the rank ordering of items crucial to survival. Amongst the items was a quart of rum. During the discussion, a lively debate ensued about the forbidden (*harram*) nature of alcohol. Some of the managers chose not to go beyond the simple truth that it was *harram* and therefore should automatically be ranked as the lowest priority. At the other extreme were the radicals who argued that in a survival situation all the rules were subordinated to the most important task of staying alive. In the middle were those who accepted that, strictly speaking, the drinking of alcohol was forbidden but argued that it would be acceptable to use it in other ways (e.g. externally, as a sterilizing agent or to start a fire).

It would be unfair to project a general orientation to new ideas from this one episode but the issue was highly symptomatic of a difference of approach that became evident on a number of occasions. There was a marked division between the managers who regarded established ideas or rules as fixed and those who felt free to re-interpret or even abandon conventional wisdom.

Staying on the Move

I have identified some of the distinguishing features of those managers whom I have labelled the Sparks, that is the people most likely to make the biggest contribution to the change initiative. There was another aspect of this group that in my view would make them successful. It was quite apparent that what had helped JANO to achieve the level of sophistication that it had attained by the time

I started working with it, was the desire to keep moving and stay ahead. The temptation to make large amounts of money from just the extraction and export of oil, until the resource was exhausted, must have been very strong.

It was hard to assess whether the Sparks would possess enough drive and restlessness to continue the process of releasing creativity described above. Certainly there were some pressures that would militate against their continuing innovation. The most powerful was the large degree of 'featherbedding' destined for them. Most of the local nationals in the group enjoyed considerable personal wealth from a number of sources. Even the less competent were guaranteed a job of some description. Featherbedding of this sort does not tend to produce the kind of restlessness necessary for continuous innovation. A second factor was that many of JANO's ideas had come from outside, that is from the foreign nationals. Although this sort of expertise was not going to dry up overnight, there was a feeling that there would be more occasions in the future when outside ideas would be ignored on the grounds of 'not invented here'.

The managers did not have to look very far for a role model of a leader who had consistently developed and innovated on a large scale. Sheikh Zayed bin Sultan al Nayhan, whose quotation heads this chapter, became the Ruler of Abu Dhabi in 1966. It was under his direction that Abu Dhabi began a massive construction programme of roads, schools, housing and hospitals from the growing oil revenues. His efforts have also earned Abu Dhabi the title of Garden City of the Gulf. It has an afforestation programme and is a net exporter of crops. However it is not just for his foresight in developing Abu Dhabi that he has become renowned. He was instrumental in persuading the seven Trucial States, as they were then known, to end their differences and join together in the federation that is today called the United Arab Emirates (UAE). Although the UAE now presents an image of co-operation and unity, this was not the case in 1971 when the federation was formed and there were many people, especially British diplomats, who were gloomy about its prospects. The quality that Sheikh Zayed seems to possess is the vision to see that the changes he was championing were not only necessary but possible. It was heartening to see that the managers held him in high regard not just because of his established ancestry but because they recognized his innovative strength.

End Case Study

CHANGE READINESS – THE BASIC PRINCIPLES

1. Looking for the Signposts

Dealing with different cultures has a lot to tell us about change readiness. It is no coincidence that amongst the list of formative experiences for a group of senior managers who were surveyed by the Centre for Creative Leadership, North Carolina, the foreign assignment was very significant for some. Managers reported having to deal with hostile left-wing governments in a language they had learned only after they had arrived there. They had to fight disease and contend with political riots.

When Peters recommends treating the customer as a foreigner he is highlighting two important factors of change readiness: listening and adapting. As he points out, 'We'd be much better off if we could pretend that our customers are foreigners who do not speak our language. They don't. Take a person who comes from the world of commercial banking. One of his customers might come from the world of contractors; the next from the world of women's wear boutiques. The language and customers are dramatically different from each other. Few of the banker's customers will speak "Banker".'

In the *Group of Managers* section of the case study, the importance of 'looking for the signposts' is highlighted. As was pointed out in the case study, signpost watching is not just a special skill reserved for dealing with foreign cultures but is something applicable to 'foreign' experiences to be found in everyday work situations.

Failure, in a new situation, to spot the signposts or even to start looking for them, can be particularly painful for the individual involved. One of our clients, a specialized steel-producing 'mini-mill', was very keen to instill in its employees the importance of close involvement with every aspect of the business. This 'hands on' approach was emphasized by the presence of the chairman on the shop floor every morning.

Involvement was seen as critical if there was a breakdown in the production process. A new foreman, witnessing such a breakdown, observed the number of men rushing to lend a hand and also identified some of their behaviour as unproductive scurrying about. His decision not to go anywhere near the problem and to stand back and observe was immediately taken by his superiors as a sign of aloofness and lack of commitment. This was a misinterpretation, however, because the new foreman had simply failed to read the signpost which said very clearly 'being seen to be involved is an important part of visibly demonstrating commitment'. Although his behaviour was in a strict sense efficient, it set him apart from his colleagues to such an extent that he found it very hard to get acceptance of some of his other ideas.

The principle of looking out for signposts at an individual level is the same one that was applied to whole organizations in the section on Strong Fuel. It is the principle of awareness of the outside environment.

2. Expecting Signposts to Move

Under conditions which are inherently changeable, it is not enough simply to read the signposts, as the section on *The Managers' Expectations* reveals. However, the fact that signposts are prone to move about can prove to be traumatic as the *Opportunities and Threats* case study indicates.

OPPORTUNITIES AND THREATS

A large organization in the financial sector decided that in order to emphasize its strategic shift towards selling, it would create a new layer of sales managers one step in the hierarchy above branch management and one step below regional management. This development was accompanied by an open and competitive selection system based on a two day assessement centre consisting of written exercises, group discussions, role play and psychometric tests. The selection method and the criteria for success on which it was based, were about as objective a means as possible of finding the best person for the job.

The end result of this new development was the successful selection of a number of high performing sales managers, accompanied by large amounts of upheaval. In the space of about six months a number of elements of the branch managers' jobs changed fundamentally. Until the introduction of the sales manager position, the company hierarchy was a very sharp pyramid with some 600 branch managers waiting for the 'dead men's' slots to be vacated by only 24 regional managers. As each region was scheduled to have four sales managers, it suddenly quadrupled the promotional chances of the branch managers. Furthermore, the criterion based assessment centre ended the old system of promotion by a 'tap on the shoulder'. Under this system, senior management made selection decisions based on their experience of the branch manager and then appointed their chosen candidate. This system tended to favour the older, often more conservative style of branch manager who had served his years without rocking the boat too much. Part of the upheaval caused by the introduction of the sales manager assessment process was that some of the managers who would have received the tap on the shoulder under the old system failed to perform adequately under assessment conditions. At the same time, some brighter, younger managers, who would have had a long wait ahead of them for promotion, succeeded at the assessment centres.

There were also some unexpected spin-offs from the assessment centre process. For the first time in the history of the organization there was a publicly available, detailed specification of what was expected of the job holder (in this case, the sales manager). Given this clarity about what was wanted, it was a simple matter for the personnel professionals to tell candidates after the assessment centres how they matched up against the criteria. Each candidate received a written report consisting of feedback on his or her performance which for most managers was probably the single largest piece of feedback they had ever received. The existing on-the-job perform-ance appraisal system was a hit and miss affair, woefully lacking in hard data and honesty.

The overall change that confronted the branch managers could be expressed as follows. It was as if the organization was saying 'Here is a new promotional opportunity and here is what we are looking for. If you want the job, you must apply for it and show us a sample of what you can do on the assessment day. The fact that you've held down your branch manager job for several years no longer works as an automatic passport'.

In one swift move they had thrown in front of them the challenge of promotion which for many of them would have been at least ten years away. They had to make an active decision about applying for the job and then gear themselves to demonstrate what they could do, in front of a panel of senior managers, during two days of high pressure scrutiny. The old ambiguity about how success was to be interpreted was swept away and the rules of the game spelled out clearly. Win or lose, they came away from the assessment process with a status report which gave them new information about their current performance and their promotional prospects.

One effect of the selection procedure described in this case study was to move one of the main signposts that the branch managers had been using as a point of reference. This made many of them suddenly feel like foreign travellers in their own home territory and with negative effects in some cases, (described in the section on Weak Air in the Air/Fuel Mixture chapter – see pages 4–8). These negative effects are not altogether surprising, when it is borne in mind that for many people, an important reference point, in pay and status terms, is the group of people with whom they identify. To relate this to the branch managers, those who weren't successful would feel suddenly deprived in relation to those who had achieved a rapid and dramatic promotion.

Despite the major threat that accompanied the opportunity described in the case study, there was a proportion of managers alert and flexible enough to get in step with the messages on the new signpost and get themselves a 'ticket' for promotion. Even amongst those who did not get their ticket the first time round, there were some who realized that there would probably be a second opportunity and that it was worth getting in step with the new system. They also recognized that all future promotions were likely to be based on the same system.

An important element of change readiness, therefore, is to expect the signposts to move. It may not be possible to anticipate the content of the message but is is usually sufficient to anticipate the fact that the movement is imminent.

3. Looking for Guides (in Unexpected Places)

The acceptance of the 'Change Really is Change' principle has already been likened to foreign travel. In any foreign travel experience there is usually a guide on hand who can provide some protection against the worst consequences of mis-reading the signposts. The same applies in an organizational setting, as the *Getting Help* section illustrates; the engineering apprentice may only have to tolerate a limited number of errands for the 'can of stripey paint' or the 'left-handed screwdriver' before a colleague or older workmate alerts him/her to the bear traps. Some organizations recognize the importance of guides, often referred to as 'mentors' at a managerial level. 'The mentoring philosophy, of nurturing the talents of tomorrow's potential top managers, is impressed down the line by the example of the chief executive and his senior colleagues . . . Grand Metropolitan's Grinstead uses the regular one-on-one meetings with operational managers behind closed doors to push, cajole and encourage them to develop increased managerial ability – and expects them to do the same down the line'.

However, the guide of the future may not always be found towards the top end of the organization. Current research data notes the emergence of flatter organizational structures, with less emphasis on the importance of hierarchy and more on the importance of specialists. When important knowledge is held by specialists situated throughout the organization, the guiding role of these individuals will become increasingly important. As far as senior managers are concerned, they are likely to continue to have an important guiding or mentoring role but seniority alone may no longer be the clue to a useful guide. Individuals with influence, the ability to 'mobilize resources' in Moss Kanter's terms, are to be found at all levels in the organization and may prove to be useful guides.

Certainly, the guiding roles altered in the organization featured in the *Opportunities and Threats* case study. Before the new selection process, a branch manager who was generally believed to be next in line for the tap on the shoulder would sometimes pass on his accumulated wisdom to a junior. Once the guarantee of promotion (under the new system) slipped away from these individuals, they were more likely to be replaced by guides who understood the new system, either by virtue of their insight or through having succeeded in the first wave of selections. Those most likely to succeed were also those who had the best grasp of the strategic forces that were driving the business and the thinking behind the appointment of sales managers. This helped to equip them as guides. The personnel specialists, who had been seriously undervalued before the change, also provided a useful guide service. Some helped managers to understand the mechanics of the new system, others provided training for aspiring candidates and a third category gave counselling to those who failed their first attempt at promotion.

There are no easy rules of thumb which dictate where to look for guides when organizations are undergoing rapid development. In the *Shifting Sands* case study, the message to emerge is the simple one of looking out for guides in unexpected places and being open to the possibility that any one of a number of individuals may prove to be useful in this role. This principle translates well into any changing organization.

4. Questioning Every Assumption
Everyone bases his actions and view of the world, to a greater or lesser degree, on assumptions. The *Releasing Creativity* section shows the importance of not getting too stuck with assumptions but rather, starting to challenge them.

The practice of questioning every assumption is one that has been well understood, for some time, by writers on creativity. One who has had a great deal of success in the practical application of his ideas to industry and commerce is an American, Roger Von Oech. The strength of his approach is that he regards almost everything as being grist to the creativity mill. His writings are presented in giant paperback form, with drawing, cartoons, one-liners and quotations as well as normal text. He exhorts his readers to use humour, metaphor, randomness and periods of doing nothing in an effort to come up with novel approaches to generating ideas. The power of Von Oech's philosophy is not simply that the solution to a creativity problem may lie in an unusual place but that the method by which the solution is reached may benefit from an unconventional approach. He questions the assumption that sitting down and thinking is the best way to analyse a problem and recommends a range of approaches which may include sampling an unfamiliar environment, such as a church for the non-church goer or the race track for a non-gambler. He even recommends being open to the idea of re-defining the problem if no solution is forthcoming, as the *Worried Skis* case study illustrates.

Case Study

THE WORRIED SKIS

We arrived for our recreational break to find that the freighting arrangements for our skis had failed to deliver and although we had snow, we had no skis. Our UK insurance company cheerily informed us that we could go ahead and buy new ones only at our own risk. In other words, if the old skis turned up while the claim was being processed, the claim would be declared void.

Feeling somewhat sour, we turned to one of our favourite books on innovative approaches to problem solving. 'Studying the inverse problem always helps; we turned our thoughts to the bizarre notion of the inverse e.g. that the skis were worrying about us turning up or that we should really worry about the risks of having too many skis rather than none at all.

Once our bad mood had subsided, we realized that there was a disguised solution in both bizarre thoughts. Although we couldn't really envisage our skis worrying about us, we could picture a scenario in which they hadn't been stolen, they had lost their identification tag and were waiting for a claimant. This led us to explore with the freight company just how hard they had tried to trace the skis back through their tortuous journey and at which stage in the process pressure should be applied for a really good search. Bizarre thought number two, of the excess of skis was, of course, a genuine possibility with the original set appearing after we had bought a new pair, but before the claim was paid. Realizing that this situation had some compensation (selling or giving to friends/ relatives or having a spare pair) made the buying decision more attractive.

The blockages to creative thinking were two-fold. There was our irritation at the situation coupled with a desire to find someone to punish for their transgression. More importantly, there was our temporary inability to recognize that looking at the inverse of the problem had produced the seeds of two possible solutions. Neither of these solutions were instantly recognizable as such, however. Their shape was ambiguous.

Under conditions of change it is productive to regard all assumptions as open to question. Rather than becoming emotionally attached to a particular way of defining a problem, to a certain type of solution or to a favoured approach to finding a solution, it is worth making the attempt to regard all avenues of exploration as potentially fruitful.

5. Not Settling Down too Quickly

When I had spent several weeks in Jebel Arabia, some of its mysteries and ambiguities began to resolve themselves and a few but not many, patterns began to emerge. The great temptation was to breathe a sigh of relief and to take the fixed points for granted. This temptation was, of course, dangerous because the internal politics meant that a change in the balance of power at the higher levels could jeopardize the work that I was doing. In fact, this change eventually came about, although not with entirely damaging effects. The temptation that I faced was paralleled by the 'featherbedding' that JANO managers would enjoy (described in *Staying on the Move*).

Even to the Spark, the keen pursuer of change, there comes the time when the thought of stability, or a period of consolidation, becomes very attractive. A number of textbooks on the subject of change refer to Lewin's model of unfreezing followed by a period of fluidity and then re-freezing. During the unfreezing state the people involved in the change process become aware of the need to tackle things differently. At first this may produce feelings of doubt, uncertainty and even hostility. As the 'unfreezing' process continues, however, they start to thaw out about the prospect of altering their ideas, opinions and behaviour. Once this has occurred then there is a readiness for the next stage which will involve an active involvement in making the new state of affairs happen. According to the model, once the change has been completed, it should be followed by a period of consolidation if it is to stick. In other words there should be a re-freezing phase.

In our view, it is the unfreezing part of the model that is most useful for many organizations. We are less confident about the possibility of or even the need for the re-freezing stage. Given our description of change as invasive, very rapid and with a random quality, the idea of an organization having time to re-freeze seems like something of a luxury.

In the *Losing Momentum* case study (below) the big failing of the company in question was to re-freeze. Some might argue that its mistake was only re-freezing too soon and that it would have needed a period of consolidation at some time. We would argue that once it had started to unfreeze, it should have stayed unfrozen.

Case Study

LOSING MOMENTUM

Our diagnosis had given us the picture of a financial services company whose success to date had been built on name, reputation and some clever opportunism that was now ten years old. It had done well enough on the seas it had been sailing so far to believe that actively steering the ship was of minor importance. The assumption was that its name, together with the inevitability of some new opportunities, would guarantee its future.

But when we looked at the charts we saw stormy seas ahead. Opportunities for expansion and new types of business were shrinking, partly due to the aggressive behaviour of competitors who targeted and pursued opportunties rather than just waiting to bump into them. There appeared to be an urgent need for some direction planning and skilled navigation.

With some misgivings, the board agreed to start its strategic planning process and to take some theoretical inputs in the form of a one week workshop/training programme. At regular intervals in the programme there were inputs on specialist topics from the tutorial team; there was also plenty of time allowed for discussion and projects based on current events in the company.

On the Friday before the Sunday on which the programme was due to begin, the personnel manager 'phoned us to say that the company was actively pursuing a merger with another organization, and she asked how should we proceed. We discussed options varying from cancellation to proceeding as planned with some extra inputs and discussion on handling mergers. As we all had a strong commitment to seeing change and growth for the company, we decided to treat the proposed merger as an opportunity and to proceed with the programme.

The week had a vibrance and an excitement that neither the personnel manager nor we had believed possible. We were fortunate in that one of our tutors, already scheduled for the programme, happened to be a merger specialist. Portions of the programme were given over to the immediate priorities posed by the new events, so instead of lecture followed by discussion, it was often lecture followed by immediate implementation of the ideas in the form of a policy paper or a circular written to all staff in the company. The climax of the week was a formal dinner at which the managing director of the other company in the deal agreed to take questions. He clearly revelled in the cut and thrust of some fairly direct questions and emerged as the hero of the hour.

By the time the second programme came round, just over a month after the first, there were some severe doubts about whether the merger could go through. What had looked like a fairly straightforward process was being threatened by rumour and rapidly swinging share prices on both sides. Before this new, less optimistic situation had arisen, we sought the advice of a senior, more experienced consultant as to how we should proceed with the second programme and subsequent follow-up. Once the doubt about the merger came to the fore he stressed to us the importance of our client company continuing to capture the energy and excitement of the first programme. He saw a danger of the company slipping back into its old ways if the merger did not go through. In his view, the merger would help the change process but was not itself the be all and end all. The change had to happen anyway.

Unfortunately not only did the merger not go through but in the ensuing anticlimax, senior managers in the company failed to keep up the momentum of change. Despite the efforts of the personnel manager and us, as consultants, the company slipped back into a 'business-as-usual' mentality. Within one year it was the subject of a hostile take-over bid and a significant proportion of its specialists and managerial talent left in two waves of resignations.

A state of permanent unfreezing may sound like a recipe for a great deal of disorder and stress. We believe that some disorder and stress is inevitable and necessary, but it is also important to have some foundations on which to stand while rapid change is taking place. In the last section of this chapter we refer to the raft of change and the concept of keeping some things constant while changing others. These constraints, in our view, are more likely to be the central values of the organization rather than events which may well change their shape and replace each other with great speed.

WHAT SHOULD REMAIN CONSTANT DURING THE PERMANENT UNFREEZING

The topic of change has been studied for some time outside the business world. For example, much has been written about how scientists go about swapping one new theory for another. There are times when science seems to leap forward because its understanding has increased several times over, as the result of a new theory. There are a number of lessons in the ways scientists behave for those of us trying to understand change in corporate organizations.

Some writers and observers regard the production of new scientific theory as a painstaking process of formulating a hypothesis, testing it against evidence and then accepting or re-formulating the hypothesis. This view earned an increasing number of opponents who wanted to capture the excitement and radical nature of the brand new theory which seemed to change the whole way in which an aspect of the natural world was analysed.

T.S. Kuhn, in *The Structure of Scientific Revolutions*, suggested an alternative view of the scientific community which looked at the revolutionary nature of some of their discoveries. In his view, the scientific community can be observed working within a frame of reference for the duration of a particular theory. This frame of reference helps scientists to look for data, analyse it and square it with their existing theory. Inevitably, some of the data does not fit the theory and over time these exceptions to the rule become so many that they cry out for a new explanation. The ill-fitting information, according to Kuhn, is waiting for a scientist with insight to 'see' things in a completely different way. For the scientist who does this, there is a revolutionary breakthrough when he/she produces a new frame of reference which captures all the previous data, ill-fitting pieces included, and explains it. There is a parallel with the picture puzzle of the young lady/old lady. We stare at the picture and can only see one of the forms, then suddenly the other aspect of the picture is revealed.

This view of the work of scientists is an attractive one and seems to account for some of the more revolutionary advances. However it is an argument which also poses a lot of problems. If taken to its extreme, it almost suggests that the scientist with the discovery has virtually to forget all that he/she has learned in order to leap into the brand new frame of reference. This is a tall order because knowledge is extraordinarily difficult to undo. When Ching-Wu Chu at the University of Houston made the discovery of 1-2-3 compound (a mix of ceramic materials) in 1987, it opened the door to superconductivity without the need for supercooling and its implications are very far-reaching indeed. However, scientists have known for 75 years that under conditions of very low temperatures certain materials can be made to conduct electricity without resistance. In a sense, Ching-Wu Chu was standing on the shoulders of all his colleagues who had previously researched the field.

The idea of revolutionary frames of reference also begs the question of what becomes of the old theory. Once in the new frame of reference, are scientists required to label what has gone before as incorrect? Again this is unsatisfactory. Old theories yield data which the new theories use and many of them continue to be useful in accounting for a whole range of natural phenomena. The ancient astronomers were able to explain and predict a number of features of the solar system which later scientists were able to confirm as being true. Although modern astronomers have discarded some of the theories of their predecessors, there is still a body of theory and a number of observations which hold true.

A leap into a new frame of reference does not necessitate completely discarding the old one. When we see the old lady in the picture puzzle it may be difficult for us to locate the young one again but with a bit of practice we can probably see both. The act of making a mental leap has been something much undervalued until relatively recently when there has been an increasing recognition of the important role of intuition.

There is a body of current research evidence which suggests that most mental functions are a complex interplay between our ability to imagine and our ability to analyse discrete pieces of data. When we look at the picture puzzle we can see the new image at the same time as being able to work out the pattern of the previous one (for example by remembering that the jaw line of the young woman translates into the nose of the old woman).

An alternative way of looking at scientific change helps to explain the phenomenon of both the old and the new co-existing. It is also a useful way of looking at organizational change, which seems to us to require the ability to live in the world of what could happen in the future, as well as in the world of what currently exists.

Our approach to change can be thought of as a raft at sea. The raft comprises a number of planks, any one of which can be replaced but not all the planks can be replaced simultaneously, for the simple reason that the occupants need something to stand on while the re-building is taking place. In terms of the development of scientific discovery there is a link between the new theory or new 'raft' and the old theory or old 'raft'. Without this link scientists who are 'seeing' things very differently from each other would not be able to communicate: they would not share any common languge in which to exchange ideas.

Science-fiction writers have a licence to describe and illustrate worlds and beings that are as different from us as it is possible to imagine. However, even in this world of extreme differences, the writers still need to create a common point of contact between the humans and the weird and wonderful beings from outer space. The aliens may have a bizarre appearance, be able to communicate with each other telepathically and ride around in flying saucers powered by a few energy cells, but in the end they have to share something in common with homo sapiens or there is no story. Often they possess the all too human feeling of a desire for world domination. With an interesting twist, Steven Spielberg in the film *Close Encounters of the Third Kind* portrayed the aliens using music and light frequencies to establish a means of communication with scientists on earth. Without this common point of contact there would have only been a short tale about the completely incomprehensible behaviour of some alien blobs.

Change may be strange to us but usually it is not completely alien. Just as the scientists venture forth into new areas of discovery standing on the raft of their previous discoveries, organizations also undergo transformation while standing on the raft of what has gone before. Even in organizations developing in many directions at a very rapid pace, what has gone before can be of vital importance. Peters and Waterman quote the example of J. Willard Marriott Sr., who, 'at eighty-two is still incensed at any sign of carelessness in a Marriott facility.' In *The Renewal Factor*, Waterman comments 'Maytag, Steelcase, IBM, all had Rock of Gibraltar values that hadn't budged a millimeter for decades . . . At other companies that renewed as a result of crises - Ryder, Ford, GE's Appliance Park - one of the early actions was to go to work on reviewing core values.'

In our own work, we have encountered organizations under-going some very important changes but at the same time hanging on to some fundamental principles and values. British Airways overcame many of its problems as an overspending part of the public sector to become a highly successful private airline. As part of the process it introduced many changes into its Engineering Depart-ment. These included new methods of working, rationalizing the size of the workforce at some levels and re-defining the roles of the first line supervisors. For some people the upheaval was consider-able, and some of the more conservative individuals questioned whether it was too much, too quickly. However, throughout this entire process, B.A. maintained its already high engineering standards, refusing to compromise on safety and winning third party contracts from other airlines to maintain their aeroplanes. When those employees who are least happy with the changes are asked why they stick to their jobs they say 'it's because we like mending aeroplanes'.

The art of maintaining a core of important values at the same time as accepting the implications of radical change is a difficult one. It is certainly one of the central issues facing the financial sector. In order to thrive in increasingly diversified and competitive markets, the financial institutions need to present a more attractive and up-beat image. This image cannot be too racy however as it would threaten to conflict with established reputations of security and sound investment.

It is not our intention to focus much attention on what organizations chose to conserve during times of change (this is already well covered in the two Waterman books referred to above). Our main interest is how to maximize the impetus and impact of new developments. However we have drawn on the metaphor of the raft in order to acknowledge that even radical change needs some kind of foundation and it is that foundation which provides us with a link to the past.

Flashpoints

CHANGE REALLY IS CHANGE

Five key elements that contribute towards readiness to change are:

- *Looking for Signposts:* this is the ability to sum up a new situation by picking up on the readily available cues and clues.

- *Expect Signposts to Shift:* during times of Ignition, the fact that a signpost said one thing one day does not mean it will say the same thing on another occasion.

- *Look for Guides in Unexpected Places:* there will be people who can provide some of the cues and clues for Ignition, but they may not be people traditionally associated with giving advice or providing such information.

- *Question Every Assumption:* all assumptions are potentially open to question. This is especially true during times of Ignition.

- *Don't Settle Down too Quickly:* what is needed is 'continuous thaw' rather than stopping and starting Ignition. Fast moving change does not have a chance to stabilize before it is nudged out of the way for the next change to start. It pays individuals and organizations not to settle down too quickly.

To help Ignition move forward, ensure that momentum is not lost, while at the same time, have respect for what needs to remain static e.g. some basic values.

REFERENCES

- Hamilton, A. (ed) (1986) *Oil – The Price of Power*, London Michael Joseph/Rainbird.

- Odell, P.R. (1986) *Oil and World Power*, Harmondsworth: Penguin.

- Peck, M.C. (1986) *The United Arab Emirates – A Venture in Unity*, London: Westview/Croom Helm.

- McHale, J. and Flegg, D. *'Innovators rule OK – or do they?'*, Training and Development October 1986.

- Kirton, M.J. *Adaptors and Innovators: A Description and Measure*, Journal of Applied Psychology, 1976.

- Runciman, W.G. (1966) *Relative Deprivation and Social Justice*, London: Routledge and Kegan Paul.

- Lombardo, M.M. *'Five Challenging Assignments'*, Issues and Observations (Centre for Creative Leadership, U.S.A.) Vol 5, No 2, May 1985.

- Peters, T.J. (1987) *Thriving on Chaos*, New York: Knopf.

- Von Oech, Roger (1983) *A Whack on the Side of the Head*, New York: Warner Books.

- Von Oech, Roger (1986) *A Kick in the Seat of the Pants*, New York: Harper and Row.

- Goldsmith, W. and Clutterbuck, D. (1984) *The Winning Streak*, London: Weidenfeld and Nicolson.

- Kuhn, T.S. (1983) *The Structure of Scientific Revolutions*, Chicago:

- Goldberg, P. (1983) *The Intuitive Edge*, Jeremy P Tarcher St. Martins Press New York.

- Neurath, O. *'Protocol Sentences'*, in Ayer A.J. (ed) (1959) *Logical Positivism*, Chicago: Free Press.

- Peters, T.J. and Waterman, R.H. (1982) *In Search of Excellence*, New York: Harper and Row.

- Waterman, R.H. (1987) *The Renewal Factor*, London: Bantam.

- Lawton, R. and Chaudhry-Lawton, R. in Livy, B. (ed) (1985) *Management and People in Banking*, London: The Institute of Bankers.

3. There Has to Be a Better Way

'I'm surprised that a government organization could do it that quickly.'
(Jimmy Carter on a visit to Egypt, on being told that it took twenty years to build the Great Pyramid)

At some stage successful Sparks, however good they are at grasping changed circumstances, will encounter resistance. As we have said in the Introduction, we are not primarily concerned with analysing the very obvious forms of resistance but it is worth looking at some of the subtle varieties which crop up frequently in several organizations. Three examples concern us in this chapter; mild acceptance, scapegoating and tuning out.

In the following case, resistance came in the surprising form of mild acceptance.

MILD ACCEPTANCE

This particular client had been thrust into the change spotlight somewhat unwillingly by a combination of factors. It occupied a conservative corner of the UK finance sector (itself not renowned for moving with the times). As a company, it was awakening to the realization that in terms of external circumstances there was trouble brewing in paradise, while internally there were some thinly disguised power struggles and grievances.

We had undertaken an in-depth diagnosis of the way in which the organization was planning strategy and how it was developing its management to cope with the strategy implementation. From a series of interviews with a cross-section of the main decision makers at the top of the company, it became apparent that there were glaring deficiencies in both the planning and implementation areas. Our written report contained a package of proposals for remedying the situation. We hoped that the package would be treated as a whole but we had also designed it so that individual elements could be worked on separately.

The chairman had read and approved the report but needed the backing of his board. He promised us a rough ride at the meeting with his colleagues asking searching questions, being openly sceptical or trying to shred the package of proposals as a means of accepting only the less radical elements.

Our job in the meeting was simply to give a brief review of the history of the project, the main reasons behind our proposals and what we were suggesting as a next step. All board members had been given the report to read in advance.

My colleague and I prepared, brainstormed the objections, reassured each other that we had done a good job, even if the proposal should be rejected, and finally we sacrificed some sleep the night before.

The next day, as our presentation ended, we were greeted with silence and polite smiles. We braced ourselves for the onslaught which never came. 'Erm, when should we start the project?' asked one board member timidly. Our main opponent, who had refused to see us during the interviews, merely sat and watched.

At the request of the chairman, we withdrew and awaited the verdict. We later learned that all our proposals had been accepted by a majority vote with our main opponent one of those in favour. When we asked for an explanation of his behaviour, the chairman told us that he was probably 'keeping his powder dry' for a later conflict. As later events were to testify, he managed to keep his powder so dry that we never actually engaged in battle. He systematically absented himself from each stage of the proposals that we had put forward, on each occasion with impeccable last minute timing. It transpired that a few of his colleagues were also members of the dry powder regiment. At various stages in the project they withdrew their support, undermined what was happening or, when forced into a corner, bared their teeth and fought. There were some supporters of the project but they were not in key positions of power or large enough in number to sway events.

In retrospect, we as consultants, together with the chairman should have forced a crisis, if not at the board meeting then shortly thereafter. At the time it felt as if gaining mild acceptance would be better than the outright rejection that we had feared. What we didn't fully appreciate was that we were working in a company culture which retained a polite equanimity on the surface but did its real knife-sharpening in more covert ways.

Perhaps one of the first questions to be asked when trying to cut through the blockages is how much those involved really want to bring about a change. In the case described above, there was a sense in which we as consultants were staying with what we knew and what was familiar. We might have felt uneasy after the board meeting but nothing like as uneasy as we would have felt if we had plucked up the courage to challenge their politeness as an unhelpful veneer.

FINDING THE SCAPEGOAT

Over-reliance on the familiar is one indicator that those involved do not necessarily want to commit themselves fully. The desire to locate a scapegoat early on may be another means of avoiding taking on the full consequences of change. Each organization will have its own favourites but common targets are the boss, the union and one or more of the service departments, such as personnel.

In one example, a group of in-house management trainers were providing a range of courses in their own company which strongly reflected their belief and interest in the human relations approach to management. They were delivering a high quality service to a mainly appreciative middle management, but were seriously under-valued by top management. Believing that access and exposure to top management would solve some of their pay, status and recognition problems, they canvassed their boss who represented them on an executive committee. At that time, he was going through a phase of being particularly de-powered, having lost many of the sources of influence that general managers at his level were accustomed to having. He did not push the cause of the trainers as powerfully as they would have wished and eventually they came to regard him as the main source of their ills.

This group were not unresourceful, however, and decided to make direct contact with the general manager responsible for most of the day-to-day business of the organization. Their aim was twofold: access to the highest level of opinion and a genuine interest in his views as to what he saw as the most pressing training needs of the business. He was sympathetic but direct and made it very clear that their management training had taken the analysis of human resource issue as far as it needed to go and that the emerging priority was business awareness for the local managers of the organization. The aim would be to help them think and act as mini entrepreneurs.

Somewhat shocked, the trainers retreated to consider their options. In the long term, the visit did not lead to a different approach to training. Instead of dealing with the new information that they had received, they chose to continue to scapegoat their own boss. It is true that much of what they criticized about him was causing their problems. However, rather than backing the alternative strategy of canvassing support elsewhere they chose not to take that rather difficult road, but instead to continue to run round the familiar circle of effort, disillusionment, blame and renewed effort.

There is good research evidence that a number of highly successful executives have actually used their 'intolerable bosses' as a source of learning, rather than as a target for scapegoating. Lombardo and McCall draw some conclusions from their findings: 'Don't take the easy way, blaming everything on that incorrigible, unethical slob. Remember that top management's evaluation of how you handle the situation may hinge on how hard you try to improve it and failing that, how you go about extricating yourself from the mess.'

Another classic scapegoat is the union. There are undoubtedly times when unions do represent a genuine obstacle to change, usually when they perceive immediately that the interests of their members are under threat. Some unions feel that the lessons of history have taught them automatically to resist new initiatives from management. A number of industrial relations experts have commented that the tendency of the right wing of the industrial management spectrum to take maximum advantage of high unemployment situations only brings about equally punitive behaviour on the part of the unions when they hold the whip hand. Unfortunately both sides continue to perpetrate the mythologies about the other side. At the time of writing, after three successive Tory governments, union membership is in decline in the U.K. The strike has been greatly undermined as a weapon and the employment legislation of the previous Labour administration is being systematically re-written in favour of the employers. In these circumstances, it is remarkable how often the unions are cited as being the main obstacle to progress in general or a new development in particular.

During a recent exploratory discussion with a union leader on the topic of a far-reaching development, referring to the management he said that, 'It's their great mistake to assume that they already know the answer, before consulting us. They either assume we will be bulldozed and proceed regardless or they give up before they've started. Both are serious mistakes.' He was reacting to what he saw as the simplistic interpretation of union motives by management. In the case of our own proposal, it would have been a serious error to see the union as an opponent that would have to be confronted or ignored.

Another common 'man of straw' that often provides the excuse for directing or delaying a change initiative is the personnel or human resources department. When it comes to the macho talk about who really runs the business or who really works at the sharp end, the human resources staff are characterized as a privileged, ineffectual group who cost money but produce little. These people can miraculously emerge at a later stage in the discussion as having the strength to block a particularly brilliant suggestion from the nitty gritty end of the business. They may be blamed for failure to recruit or train sufficient numbers of employees or for their over-adherence to legislation. Some human resource departments, therefore, go from Cinderella, to the giant in charge of the beanstalk in the space of a few minutes. Of course some departments earn their reputations at both ends of the spectrum. As Moss Kanter points out, the human resource specialists, starved of access to the organizational power lines, may respond by grabbing the only power they have access to, which is the restrictive power to block innovation by reference to professional or departmental boundaries.

The method of dealing with the barrier presented by any specialist department is first to question how real the barrier is and secondly, as with the union example, get as close to the source of the problem as possible. Real dialogue with the service department helps to soften the stereotype and may invigorate its staff by allowing them access to the organizational power lines (in Moss Kanter's terms, supplies, support and information). Heavy handed use of restrictive power is often a sure sign that the individual or department in question feels insecure and lacking in real influence. Rather than dismissing this behaviour as petty minded, it may be more productive to reduce the level of threat and insecurity by showing some of the rewards that the new development may bring.

We have examined so far, two reasons why obstacles and resistance to change may not be effectively tackled by people who basically do want something new to happen. The attraction of the familiar and the security that it provides may leave people paddling in the shallows rather than striking out for the deep end. The ease with which a scapegoat can be created may provide an opportunity for doing the same thing, that is, not venturing into new territories because it is more comfortable to continue to blame the boss, the unions, or one of the service departments. Creating a scapegoat or staying in familiar surroundings are both essentially defence mechanisms. There are times when defence mechanisms feel very necessary to those involved in a new development. Sometimes people allow barriers to change to stay in the way, simply because things are happening so rapidly that they need time to think.

TUNING OUT

The modern manager and specialist potentially has immediate access to data through computer networks, telex, telephone (including paging devices and cellular mobile systems) and facsimile machines. Should he/she choose, all these systems can be brought into the home which may already have a television with a telex system and a video cassette recorder. As a number of commentators have pointed out, the issue now becomes one of selection, rather than supply of information.

Selection under pressure creates its own particular stresses and strains. America's top military pilots who fly 'electronic offices' through the sky at incredible speed report the phenomenon of overload. They have a huge amount of information coming in very fast and requiring decisions (attack the enemy, take evasive action, reposition etc). In certain situations pilots apparently 'tune out' by literally switching off some of the inputs or by mentally switching off.

The everyday corporate parallel occurs when people start to adjust the pressure of decision-making at work to one that they can cope with. If they are in the middle of a new development which bombards them with a large volume of unfamiliar data, a temporary hitch or delay can appear as a gift from heaven. The phenomenon of controlling pace of work has long been recognized amongst production line workers. We have had direct experience of this in a local soft drinks factory. Dirty bottles were loaded on to a conveyor belt, processed through a washing machine, quick dried, filled with the brew of the day, capped and conveyed off the line ready for loading into crates. On more than one occasion, the management took the unilateral decision to increase productivity by speeding up the line. Each time this was attempted, the stress on all the operators increased and one of them would engineer a well disguised 'accident'. The most spectacular incident involved tilting several of the dirty bottles from the vertical so that they started to arrive in the washer at anything but the correct angle. During the ensuing chaos of broken glass and grinding machinery, most of the operatives found that they had sudden appointments with the washroom.

Except in truly adversarial situations, such as the one described above, most managers and specialists do not 'tune out' with the deliberate aim of causing the whole system to break down. If they are in the middle of pushing for change, they may simply start to pursue it with less vigour or allow one of the barriers to remain in place until they are capable of re-engaging with the struggle.

Although 'tuning out' can be a rational survival strategy, it does rely on the 'tuner' knowing what is surplus to requirements. The American pilots who reported on how they switched instruments off were alive to tell the tale. One of them, however, reported a near miss when he failed to recognize the verbal input of one of his crew amongst all the other data he was receiving. A tape-recording of the episode revealed a clear verbal warning of approaching enemy aircraft, but the pilot reported not hearing it because his attention was focused on a battery of incoming electronic data.

The process of 'tuning out', therefore, appears to be one which is necessary from time to time but presents two kinds of danger to the change process. Vital data may be tuned out and failure to react to it may threaten the new development. A tendency to 'tune out' may go beyond a safety mechanism and actually become a habit. If it becomes a pattern then we can list it, along with staying with the familiar and scapegoating, as a change avoidance technique.

Staying with the familiar, scapegoating and erroneous 'tuning out' are pitfalls which could trip up any individual or group of individuals who are moderately keen to move forward but who haven't made the full commitment. Some people seem to possess the Spark quality that naturally enables them to cut through the resistance and get to their goal. This quality may come in different forms. We have come across the head-on, high confrontation variety, the occasional switch-on of power (sometimes in unexpected ways) and the maverick who has the knack of finding organizational obstacles to bump into or knock over.

The Head-On Approach

A friend of mine, Nick, clearly loves the head-on approach and likes to race cars in his spare time and to drive performance cars in the course of his business. Realizing that he was not unique in this interest he examined the behaviour of the salesmen for whom he was responsible. To his dismay he found that although they were required to carry heavy samples in the boot, they were driving their fleet cars in a way that would have made Mansell gulp. Naturally this was having some fairly serious consequences for the car engines. Overnight he came up with the master stroke of re-equipping the entire fleet with diesel-powered equivalents that ensured an end to dramatic attempts to accelerate hard. Although Nick was not popular for this radical change in fleet car policy, all the salesmen understood that he had enough knowledge of the business not to be fooled into thinking that the mechanical failures were the result of some mysterious fault in the original car.

On another occasion, Nick again demonstrated his ability to meet his staff on their own territory. One of the salesmen had produced consistently bad results but claimed nevertheless that his activity level was high and that he was always on the road by 8 o'clock in the morning. Nick was not convinced but had something of a dilemma as the salesman in question lived nearly 200 miles away. Having tried long-distance counselling over the phone, Nick decided that there was nothing for it but to make an early start himself one morning. He arrived outside the salesman's home at 7.30 a.m. and waited patiently. The wait actually lasted until 9.30 a.m., the time at which his subordinate eventually emerged. In taking this action, Nick has broken a few rules about not spying on subordinates. He did however rescue the salesman's career who, without the plain talking he heard from Nick at 9.30 a.m. in the morning, would have been on his way out of the company.

Other managers we have seen operate are perhaps more tactical than Nick but nevertheless are capable of carrying the Spark which is at the centre of the Ignition. They seem to know when it is worth taking the risk and usually carry some insurance against disaster if they feel very close to the edge. Their exposure to risk is likely to be for a limited time period so in effect they are doing what has been referred to below as 'pulsing' or pushing their influence in brief bursts.

PULSING

Colin is quite unlike Nick but nevertheless has created the necessary Spark on a number of occasions. Some of the time he appears conservative and dutiful. He likes to work hard but is a meticulous keeper of a time management system and has very strict cut-off points for meetings and schedules. Yet perhaps his first love is to study and teach creativity.

His eyes twinkle at the thought of an unusual idea and he is excited by new projects. For many years he has worked in an organization which has been both attracted by his new ideas and shocked by their radical nature. In the early days it was probably more shocked than pleased and Colin learnt how to push one of his more adventurous schemes. The technique of storing credits by conventional behaviour in order to make his unconventional ideas more acceptable has worked well for him and ultimately earned him some conventional but powerful recognition.

Interestingly, Colin had a variety of ways of cashing in his credits and they were not always connected with creative ideas. On one memorable occasion he decided to have a showdown with his boss whose management style was probably more akin to that of Nick's in the earlier example. Although the wall shook with the sound of raised voices, it appeared that Colin had judged his showdown correctly and was able to return unscathed from his own particular 'high noon'. In his terms there were enough credits in his bank for his shouting match not to push him into the red.

Although hard to define, the Spark quality in a person is often easy to recognize. We had spent two weeks running a management skills programme for a group of international bankers. With this particular group we had found ourselves having to fight every inch of the way. A number of them resented having to work over a residential weekend and the majority found any analysis of behaviour tantamount to an assault on their psyches. It was almost as if they saw themselves as the Thin Red Line fighting off the Zulus. In a sense this was true, because although we hadn't realized it, they thought of themselves as the beleaguered garrison of old style managers, holding out against the invasion of changes in the finance sector. When the invasion actually arrived during our training fortnight, it came in the form of one of their colleagues from the foreign exchange division.

He was younger than the average member of the group and wore a suit which took the ambiguous path between respectable enough for work but sharp enough for a London nightclub. Not in the least put off by the ostentatious surroundings of the college in which we were working, he strode into the bar, dropped his slim attaché case and said in his best cockney accent 'Nice 'ere init? – I'll 'ave a pint!' His gin and tonic drinking colleagues looked aghast.

Once he started his after-dinner talk, his colleagues were both aghast and charmed. His presentation sparkled and crackled with humour as well as conveying the excitement and pace of his work.

After the invader had left, a grim, square-jawed member of the group came up to me and ruefully admitted, 'That's where the future of our business lies, with him, not with people like me'. For a brief period our visitor had created a Spark of enlightenment amongst the group and had done a great deal towards making the group more receptive to our messages.

Our final category of Spark is the maverick. Mavericks tend to produce unusual and creative ideas and methods of working wherever they are. If they happen to be in an organization that can harness their talents then their outputs will have an organizational focus, but they are rarely motivated solely by the desire to achieve the greater corporate good. Even when their energies are diverted towards a corporate aim they usually accompany their labours with a measure of humour, or a flouting of rules, or an idiosyncratic personal style guaranteed to jar with their surroundings.

THE MAVERICK

Mr. Bubbly was a middle-grade public sector administrator. He looked like the comedian Jimmy Edwards, but with a hint of malevolence thrown in. His name gave him a great deal of delight and others much consternation, for his favourite trick was to answer a phone call with the simple word 'Bubbly' (was this a comment, an insult, a request for champagne or his name?) Mr. Bubbly's management style was mock military, with bluff and bluster mixed with a great deal of humour. He was competent, but lazy.

Early in his career, Mr. Bubbly had his promotional prospects blighted when he wrote a script for an in-house film and performance appraisal. The script was peppered with real life examples drawn from senior management but so thinly disguised that they were immediately able to identify themselves. Organizational legend had it that the film mysteriously disappeared and a permanent note appeared on Mr. Bubbly's file. Certainly he was never promoted again.

Mr. Bubbly found himself in a state of suspended animation, haunted by the albatross of the film. He used his position to good effect, and as a member of the Establishments Division responsible for career development of white collar staff across the organization, he single-handedly set up a clearing house system. The system was based on a complex series of deals and trades. A division of the organization which had a vacancy could rely on Mr. Bubbly to supply a suitable candidate, on the understanding that on a future occasion they might have to contribute one of their own people for promotion or transfer to another division in need. Every division owed Mr. Bubbly a favour. He kept the velocity of circulation high, and individuals prepared to move job and sometimes location could expect a good many sideways moves and promotions. They benefited tremendously and so did the organization.

Miraculously, Mr. Bubbly never committed anything to paper but chose instead to carry the whole system in his head. This was miraculous on two counts. The system was very complex and very finely balanced. Perhaps more importantly, he was working in a vast bureaucracy which worshipped paper, duplicate and triplicate copies, filing systems, precedents and procedures. It was as if Mr. Bubbly had struck an informal deal with the organization that if it was never going to promote him he would create his own job. He was determined to do the job effectively, but en route wanted to wave two fingers at the organization's procedures.

Some people could not handle Mr. Bubbly's inconoclastic style while others seemed actually to enjoy it and joined in with his personal joke. One senior manager loved nothing more than to introduce Mr. Bubbly as 'Mr. Green' to an important guest, just to hear Mr. Bubbly correct the mistake and reveal his real name.

The Spark who is also a maverick can be of as much value to the organization as the other types mentioned. One difference may be that they come with a different kind of price label attached. In cases such as these, organizations have to tolerate some patterns of behaviour which mock or openly reject some of the corporate values.

SPARKS AND THE PUBLIC SECTOR

We have witnessed examples of Sparks in the public sector in the same way as we have witnessed them in the private sector. When I joined the Greater London Council (GLC) in 1976 it had a large number of young, energetic, competent managers who were action orientated and would have had no problems translating their skills into industrial and commercial practice (some of them did). The Council was attracting visitors from all over the world to see two innovative projects; the Thames Barrier and the Edmonton incinerator plant. Now completed, the Thames Barrier is a bold feat of civil engineering, designed to prevent most of the East End and large parts of central London from vanishing in the event of the increasingly likely occurence of a flood, driven by winds backing a spring tide. Huge curved gates lie dormant on a wide stretch of the river at Silvertown allowing shipping to pass but capable of being raised in the event of a flood.

The Edmonton incinerator plant is a vast furnace capable of burning the majority of household refuse and using the heat generated to produce electricity via steam turbines. Not only was the GLC a public works innovator, it also had terms and conditions for its staff which predated many of the developments incorporated in the employment legislation of the mid 1970s. Yet at the same time, the enormous budget of the GLC (said to exceed the spending power of the Swedish National Government) and some of its profligate spending attracted a barrage of criticism. So much so, that a decade later its drain on resources, coupled with a very provocative Labour leadership under Ken Livingstone, became more than Margaret Thatcher could bear and she dissolved the Council by Act of Parliament. In doing so she admittedly stopped a source of over-spending but at the same time she also destroyed an organization which had the capacity to integrate and innovate across the boundaries of warring London boroughs.

It seems to be a feature of much of the public sector that the good and the bad, in terms of management and corporate practice, become inextricably linked together. There were times when the GLC could be a ridiculous hierarchy of staffing grades arranged in narrow categories of professional, technical, administrative and clerical. It had abandoned some of the labelling of the military model used in a previous era (some administrative grades were called 'Regulars' which, when coupled with their lettering system, meant a person could be the proud holder of the title 'Regular B'). Much to the amusement of newcomers such as myself, it did not abandon the habit of referring to sections of one particular department as blocks, conferring upon the leader the illustrious title of 'block head'.

One of the legends circulating when I joined was that the Housing Department had achieved its over-manning by a quirk of fate at the previous round of staff budgeting. Fearing cuts, the department doubled its bid for staff, expecting to have the bid halved. The bid was accepted at face value. Undoubtedly, the story is apocryphal but most people believed that something like that must have happened.

It is within the grasp of all organizations, public sector or not, to do away with the kinds of abuse outlined above. However the public sector does face a number of problems in operating the kind of Ignition model that we are proposing. Perhaps one of the biggest considerations is that of accountability to the public. Many of the rules that govern public sector systems are there to ensure that public funds are not squandered or embezzled.

An acquaintance of mine who joined the civil service was very able and highly individualistic in his approach. Being very short and double-jointed in many places he found the office seating arrangements far too restrictive. Rumour had it that on occasion he would take his work underneath his desk and sit there. Apparently his superiors valued his work sufficiently to permit this to continue. Work was not the only thing going on under his desk, however. On one occasion he revealed to me that he had 'rescued' a juvenile offender who had fallen foul of the workings of the judicial and penal systems. As he described the case, the youth in question was being victimized as an accidental spin-off of some clumsy bureaucratic procedures. When I asked him how he had managed to get the youth more lenient treatment he explained that he placed the boy's file behind the radiator and declared it 'lost' in the system. I was both pleased and shocked by the example. Pleased because my Lone Ranger acquaintance had intervened in the working of an unfair system but shocked because I realized that if he could 'lose' files so could other civil servants whose values and opinions I might not share. In the event of this latter group of people seizing the power to 'lose' files I would find myself amongst the group clamouring for rules and restrictions.

The accountability issue is one which is often quoted by public sector bodies when they are under attack. They will point out that their critics in the private sector have, in comparison, far more freedom to act. Even the demands of shareholders impose far fewer constraints than those of the elected representatives of the public as a whole.

This is an argument that is difficult to sustain in the face of increasing responsiveness on the part of a number of organizations to the needs and demands of the community. In their survey of Britain's top companies, Goldsmith and Clutterbuck note, 'Where integrity comes into play most effectively in dealings with the external world is in responsiveness to significant moral issues. Successful companies will not risk the good currency of the corporate brand name by ignoring strong moral public feeling. By the same token, they appreciate the value to the maintenance of the brand name of being associated with responsible and caring behaviour . . . Marks & Spencer, Sainsbury and United Biscuits are typical of the inner core of successful companies who see the benefits of a pro-active stance on social issues. They attack these issues with the same intensity and planning that they put into other significant management tasks'.

One of Clive Thornton's policies as chief executive of the Abbey National Building Society was to put it on the map as an integral part of the community. Although the British building society movement as a whole has a reputation as a paternalistic inheritor of the values of the old friendly societies, it had, for many years, been wary of offering home loans on properties in areas of inner city decay. This practice of 'red lining' as it was known, was clearly at odds with any attempts to stimulate growth in the inner cities and also at odds with the caring image that the building society supposedly had. Thornton, convinced that the success of any organization was partly a function of its standing in the community, decided to tackle the urban regeneration problem in three ways. He established a housing association under the wing of the Abbey National to provide houses and flats at economic rent for low income groups and people with special needs. The criteria for lending in the inner cities were relaxed and he appointed one of his own managers to the team of politicians and industrialists investigating inner city problems, folowing the unrest in areas such as Toxteth in Liverpool.

It is undoubtedly true that at the same time as creating some socially responsible policies, Thornton was also making a shrewd business move. His innovations raised his own public profile and that of the Abbey National. The policies were very much in harmony with those of the ruling Tory government at a time when there was a Green Paper which proposed freeing some of the restrictions on building societies at the same time as ending some of their privileges. Inner city purchases were never going to be big business, but the 1980 Housing Act did give tenants of council and housing association property the right to buy their own homes and naturally the Abbey National was well placed to provide some of this funding. Finally, the creation of the Abbey National housing association established the principle, for the first time, of a building society being able to own property other than its own business premises.

The argument about whether or not socially minded policies in the private sector are just good business practice is a complex one. It is true that some of the more socially responsible organizations are led by people who have high ethical standards which they have held for a number of years and which they also practice in their private lives. At the same time these individuals are good businessmen who can afford to distribute some largesse. In reference to their Marks & Spencer, Sainsbury and United Biscuit examples, Goldsmith and Clutterbuck go on to say 'they can afford to put something back into society because they are immensely profitable'. The implication here is that their standing in the community is one of the things that makes them profitable so that they can continue to put back into society and maintain their reputation.

Whatever the motivational basis for socially responsible busiesses, their existence means that public sector organizations are not the only ones with public accountability. Indeed, there is a good argument which says that even private sector organizations who are reluctant to accept social responsibility may have this role thrust upon them. The authors of *Super-Managing* comment 'The public is increasingly holding *all* institutions to a higher standard of accountability these days. This even applies to TV networks when the issue is violence on TV as it affects children and to non-profit research laboratories when the issue is the dearth of results from the National Cancer Institute's $8 billion for cancer research'. They go on to point out that the area in which business decisions are taken is becoming increasingly visible and filled with groups holding a stake in the outcome: 'Managers, especially those in senior positions should learn to be more comfortable with decision making in a fishbowl. Given the fact that employees, the press, stakeholders and special-interest groups will continue to clamour for increased disclosure, some types of closed-door decisions that are made without involving the affected parties could be disastrous'. Some companies who have ignored stakeholders have found that they can be held accountable whether they like it or not. Thus Coca–Cola found itself agreeing to channel more than $30 million to black businesses as a result of the Reverend Jesse Jackson's operation PUSH initiating a 'selective' buying campaign.

Sometimes the accountability argument is buried in a larger discussion about the importance of values, generally, in the public sector. It has been argued that the public sector cannot really be expected to perform in the same ways as comparable private sector organizations because they cherish a number of values which are not linked to the profit motive. A chief executive of a public body once told me that he feared he would not benefit from a training course offered to chief executives in all sectors of the economy because his peers would not understand what it meant to be head of a value-driven organization. Playing devil's advocate, I informed him that he would find that Derek Hunt, the Chief Executive of MFI, would understand the importance of values in the business very well indeed. This was not just advocacy on my part, as I had first hand experience of the effects that the values of hard work and commitment were having on MFI managers. At a later stage, the book *The Winning Streak* bore this out; ' . . . severe snow at York blocked all roads. The staff all turned up even though the customers couldn't get there,' says Hunt. 'They sold one coffee table at £9.95!'

As an argument why some public sector organizations fail to perform, their adherence to a set of non-profit driven values does not seem to be a valid one. This is particularly the case in view of the mounting volume of literature already quoted in this book (*In Search of Excellence, The Winning Streak, The Change Masters, The Renewal Factor*) which supports the argument that value-driven organizations in the private sector often do best.

If the values argument alone does not account for some of the private sector/public sector differences, then it is worth examining another theory that is put forward from time to time. It has often been said that in the area of service to the public, some of the work carried out is very difficult to measure. Customer satisfaction may rarely be reported and in some cases may happen at a time and place well removed from the original supplier. For example, young students may well not recognize the benefit of the formative education that they have received until they start work or move on to higher education, several years later. Without measurable results, the argument goes, it is hard to produce tangible rewards related to the performance of employees who provide the service.

Again, a close examination of some private sector organizations reveals that they too have to confront the problems faced by their counterparts in the public sector. The number of private organizations in the service sector is large and growing. Many of them have discovered that in the absence of really good measures of customer satisfaction or employee performance in relation to that satisfaction, an attempt at measurement is better than no measurement at all. The Strong Fuel Section of the Air/Fuel Mixture (see pages 18 - 23) highlights the efforts that some chief executives are prepared to go to in order to obtain customer information, and also details some of the more novel ways of checking the customer's pulse (B.A.'s video booths, for instance).

The strong message going out from a number of successful companies is the urgent need to canvass customer opinion regularly and to use whatever measures come to hand. This includes treating customer opinion and feelings as important data and not just dismissing them as irrelevant 'subjectives'. There is no reason why this cannot also be done by public sector organizations. Peters quotes an example from the Police Department of Santa Barbara, California, where Lieutenant Greg Stock pushed his officers to get direct contact with the public; 'The officers just ring a few doorbells every day, introduce themselves, give out a "business card" with emergency phone numbers and encourage citizens to call for any reason.'

Measurement of employee performance is not something which is new to the public sector, certainly in the UK. It was interesting to hear the howls of pain, however, when it was proposed that a performance appraisal system should be introduced for teachers. Again, the unsophisticated argument surfaced that because teachers did not manufacture products but dealt instead in concepts and ideas, their performance could not be measured. Those supporting this view overlooked the fact that reasonably sophisticated performance appraisal systems have for decades now enabled competent bosses to observe behaviour in relation to established criteria of performance and to gauge its relative effectiveness. That which is quantifiable in numerical terms is thought by many to be only part of an employee's performance. Increasing attention is being paid to intangibles such as commitment and team membership.

The complexity of the measurement problem in parts of the public sector should not be denied, however. For example, in the National Health Service, the application of cost/benefit analysis is fraught with problems. A unit of expenditure on, for example, an operation has both an output (say, an hour of a nurse's time) and an outcome (the hoped for improvement in a patient's health). Whereas an output may be fairly predictable, an outcome will not be in all cases (the patient may not improve). Outcomes also have a value judgement implied. This raises the question of whether the operation has been 'worth it' if it only brings about temporary remission from pain and, of course, this depends on who is asking the question (the patient's point of view may differ from that of the health economists). The difficulties associated with this kind of analysis should not be ducked. In the final analysis, there is only a finite amount of resource available and it has to be allocated somehow.

Ever since the Tory government came to power in the UK in 1979 one of its keen interests has been to stimulate greater efficiency and entrepreneurial behaviour in the public sector. This has been mixed with other motivations including the desire to lessen government interference and to widen the base of share ownership amongst the general public. When the topic of privatization is being debated it is often around the efficiency question that the argument is centred. It is this debate that is of particular relevance in this chapter. In terms of the Ignition metaphor, the supporters of privatization would claim that Spark-like behaviour is only really stimulated by the commercial pressures of privatization.

IS IGNITION POSSIBLE WITHOUT PRIVATIZATION?

The supporters of the privatization of public services argue that it is a necessary pre-condition of dramatic improvement and organizational change. Critics of the current operation of the public sector in the UK are able to point to ill-defined or non-existent standards of performance and service, inefficiencies, and a treatment of customers which can range from indifference to downright hostility.

Administrators in one area health authority reported a long-standing complaint that some consultants would book more time in the operating theatres than they had the intention of using in order to maintain their image. In his launch of a proposed citizens' charter in July 1991, John Major was able to capture some immediate public support when he referred to the abuse of booking systems by hospital administrators. Many people have experienced the frustration of an over-long wait in the outpatients' department because several people have been booked in at the same time. In principle, this is designed to ensure a steady flow of patients to the consultant but the solution wildly over-compensates for the problem of missed appointments. The problems are not confined to the health service and the areas for improvement identified by Major in his proposals are all too familiar to people of all political persuasions in the UK. At one end of the scale are mundane issues such as motorway lanes unnecessarily coned-off for long periods and the problem of the failure of utilities servicemen to give and keep appointment times. Some of the larger scale issues include the waste and frustration caused by late trains and disconnected services and the failings of the postal services.

Waste and inefficiency in the public sector is not exclusively the result of mismanagement or indifference. Sometimes it is the product of an over-elaborate set of rules designed to protect public money, as the next case study illustrates.

A RUBBISH REWARD

The council depot gathered household refuse for an urban district, scraped it into a huge pile and shipped it out to a landfill site, somewhere in the countryside. Wear and tear on the huge tractor doing the scraping was very heavy. Chunks of metal and shards of glass abounded.

The operatives possessed large amounts of native wit. For example, many of them ran sideline businesses in 'totting' or salvaging scrap metal. The link between creativity and native wit is a close one. In order to prevent rapid deterioration of their tractors they grafted on various modifications.

At the time, the local council had a staff suggestion scheme. For a good suggestion it would pay out a maximum of £250, following written reports and the deliberations of a panel. Really good suggestions could attract a higher reward but only with reference to the panel, plus senior officer, plus elected members of the council. The tractor modifications were saving the council something in excess of £2,000 per annum. In the time it took the staff suggestions to be processed, the company manufacturing the tractors had seen the early modifications and started incorporating them into their designs.

The slowness of the staff suggestion scheme greatly frustrated the operatives. They threatened to patent their ideas. At this point, the council swiftly countered by pointing out that ideas generated during paid time were the council's property. During this long period of stalemate the bad feeling generated on all sides completely negated the eventual benefits of the staff suggestion scheme's award. A modest payment, a little more than £250, would have satisfied the operatives' needs. It was recognition they sought, not just money.

The view of the pro-privatization lobby is that many of the problems of a complacent and unchallenged public sector start to evaporate once the prospect of market pressure and shareholder demands start to emerge. It is certainly true that a number of organizations have been able to drive through some quite radical change immediately before and after privatization. The British Airways example is a classic. More recently, London Buses have made a number of changes in advance of full deregulation. These include ending some inefficient practices and thus cutting unit costs, the appointment of a marketing director and setting up training schemes in passenger care for the driver/operators of one-person operated buses.

However privatization alone does not guarantee that Ignition-driven change will take place. A number of the services privatized in the late 1980s and early 1990s have still held near monopoly positions, and have therefore not felt some of the market pressures deemed to be so healthy for them. The comparative weakness of the regulatory bodies has been the source of considerable criticism. In the case of British Telecom, for example, its sole incentive to charge Mercury, its long-distance rival, reasonable rates for access to local networks, is the presence of the regulatory agency OFTEL. Ultimately, British Telecom knows more about its own cost structure than OFTEL does, which makes the incentive to fair play only a weak one. It is significant that part of Major's citizens' charter is the strengthening of the three regulatory bodies OFTEL, OFWAT (Water) and OFGAS.

Once public services have been privatized, there may well be a need for greater regulation and intervention than would normally be the case in the rest of industry and commerce. A number of people, for example, expressed concern before the privatization of the water boards that standards would not be maintained. Even in the UK's heartland of privatization, the City, there were some doubts. As one commentator put it, 'Maggie's (Thatcher) army of capitalists . . . is more interested in worm-free water than a turn on the EC2 casino (London Stock Exchange)'. This concern has been borne out recently (post privatization) by incidents such as the release of unsafe water into the supply to the west of London. The problem was compounded by the delay in informing the authorities and the public. The water companies are currently at the centre of the controversy about the failure of Britain's beaches to reach EEC standards of cleanliness. A Consumers' Association report shows a failure on the part of many beaches to satisfy standards for viral contamination. The government response is to challenge the standard as unreasonable and not to put pressure for reform on the water companies.

It is not surprising that the government that has been the driving force behind privatization has also embraced the policy of laissez-faire and an avoidance of trying to regulate closely newly privatized companies. The two policies may not be compatible, however, for the reasons already explored. The chief danger of not intervening is the creation of the frightening combination of a monopoly supplier of public services, driven by the profit motive. Opponents of privatization, such as the Labour Party, are quick to point out what they see as abuses carried out by the privatized utilities (for example excessive costs, including massive salary increases for directors).

If intervention and regulation has such a vital role to play after privatization, this opens up a second possibility for trying to stimulate Ignition in the public sector. By regulating, legislating and encouraging existing services to behave as if they were privatized, while maintaining them in the public sector, it may be possible to promote change without losing the concept of public service. Many of the citizens' charter proposals are aimed in this direction. There is no reason why public servants should not be expected, in Major's words 'to identify themselves to the public, with the giving of names on the telephone or in letters and, where appropriate by the wearing of badges'. In the event of failures and complaints there is a need for 'well-signposted avenues for complaints if the customer is not satisfied, with some independent review wherever possible'. Perhaps most importantly, it is proposed that a chartermark would be obtainable by services able to maintain and define 'standards of service that the customer can reasonably expect and of performance against those standards'.

Standards, accountability and the legitimate right of complaint accompanied by compensation are central to the charter proposals. In the education sphere, schools would be required to publish results in the local press, to publish truancy rates and to have an independent inspectorate. On the railways, staff would have performance pay based on attendance and punctuality and there would be compensation for poor service for season ticket holders and Inter-City users. In the health service, proposals cover maximum times for treatment, timed appointments for all outpatients and the publication of a national league table on hospital efficiency.

The Key Role of Intervention

The privatization lobby has gained strength partly because many of the public services left to their own devices have appeared to be incapable of fundamental change. In terms of the model outlined in *The Air/Fuel Mixture* (page x) they have remained in a *Weak Fuel/ Weak Air* environment.

Stimulating Ignition in organizations is, by its very nature, an interventionist activity. Privatization is a type of intervention and one which carries great potential for bringing about change. However, in the case of many of the public services, the need for the government to regulate and intervene often continues beyond privatization in order to prevent the abuse of monopoly power.

If privatization alone doesn't automatically free the public services from the trap of *Weak Fuel/Weak Air* and if regulation and legislation is going to be necessary post privatization, this raises the possibility of keeping a number of services in the public sector but intervening to bring about change. In many ways, the citizens' charter is an attempt to achieve precisely that objective. It may well be that in order to be successful, the government has to go beyond the principles outlined in the charter. For example, many of the public services are seriously underfunded in relation both to what they are required to do and to their counterparts in other countries. If the citizens who are the key concern of the charter do not have access to relevant information then they cannot challenge some of the weaker areas of the public services. In the words of one commentator, 'We will be allowed to know whether the trains are cleaned but not what safety problems the railway inspectorate have discovered'.

The privatization debate has unnecessarily polarized thinking about change in the public sector. It is interesting that immediately prior to the privatization of the water companies, some people drew attention to the French example where public provision and private supply sit side by side. In France most water supply assets, such as pipes, pumps and treatment stations, are owned by the municipalities. French water companies compete directly with one another for long-term contracts to operate the supply. The system is regulated locally by municipalities which set the price to be paid by the consumers in direct contract negotiations with the company. The municipality can dispense with the water company and operate the supply itself, if it is dissatisfied.

Bringing about Ignition using privatization is only one fairly blunt instrument for generating change and without continuing regulation for new monopoly supplies loses its impact or even works in a contrary way. If regulation is to be a feature of public sector life, intelligent intervention can be used to promote change. In some situations the ideal combination from the end users' point of view might be a mix of public and private sector provision. There is an urgent need for a better understanding of the organizational changes that have to take place in the public sector so that a better understanding can then inform the debate about public or private provision.

There has to be a Better Way

Resistance to Ignition can take many forms. Three common defence mechanisms are:

- *Mild Acceptance:* in this case, attraction of the familiar and the security that it provides may leave people paddling in the shallow end rather than striking out for the deep end.

- *Finding a Scapegoat:* the ease with which a scapegoat can be created may provide an opportunity for doing the same thing rather than change i.e. not venturing into new territories because it is more comfortable to blame the boss, the unions or one of the service departments (such as personnel).

- *Tuning-Out:* vital data may be 'tuned out' and failure to react to it may threaten Ignition. A tendency to tune out may harden into a habit or a change avoidance technique.

Different Sparks
- Sparks cut through resistance. There are those who overcome obstacles by tackling them head-on, by acting with bursts of energy ('pulsing') or the mavericks who have the knack of finding obstacles to bump into or knock over.

Ignition and the Public Sector
- The manager operating in the public sector has to be aware of the issue of public accountability. This does not place him/her in a unique position, as parts of the private sector are increasingly being held accountable. It should not be used as an excuse for avoiding reasonable risks.

- Although the effects and efficiency of many public sector services are hard to measure it is not an impossible task. The private sector has shown the way in a number of areas which at first sight look highly ambiguous and difficult to define. Some public sector organizations have already found new and creative ways of measuring customer satisfaction and it is worth developing this trend.

- If privatization creates a near monopoly supply in an environment lacking government monitoring and regulation, it is unlikely that the profound change implied by the Ignition model will take place. This implies some form of intervention, but, there is no reason why intervention could not be introduced into services which are kept within the public sector. The issue is not so much public versus private but how to get the best level of service from a limited amount of resources.

REFERENCES

- Lombardo, M.M. and McCall Jr., M.W. *'The Intolerable Boss'*, Psychology Today, January 1974.

- *'Unions ready to go on offensive after Weathering Storm'*, Personnel Management, December 1987.

- *'How Personnel can lose its Cinderella Image'*, Personnel Management, December 1987.

- Moss Kanter, R. *'Power Failure in Management Circuits'*, Harvard Business Review, July–August 1979.

- Naisbitt, J. (1984) *Megatrends*, New York: Warner.

- *'Top Gun and Beyond'*, Transcript from PBS NOVA (broadcast January 19, 1988) WBGH Educational Foundation, Boston, Mass.

- Brown, A. and Weiner, E. (1984) *Super-Managing*, Maidenhead: McGraw-Hill/Mentor.

- Holden, J. *'Fox Hunting'*, Industrial Marketing, June 1982.

- Goldsmith, W. and Clutterbuck, D. (1984) *The Winning Streak*, London: Weidenfeld and Nicolson.

- Peters, T.J. and Waterman, R.H. (1982) *In Search of Excellence*, New York: Harper and Row.

- Peters, T.J. (1987) *Thriving on Chaos*, New York: Knopf.

- *'An Imprecise Science'*, The Health Service Journal, August 1988.

- *'Major Spells Out His Plan For The Decade'*, Independent 23 July 1991.

- *'Consumer Rights "To Be Central Theme of 1990s" '*, Independent 23 July 1991.

- *'The Regulatory Two-Step'*, The Economist 21 January 1989.

- *'Water: Thatcher and Ridley Take a Bath'*, Observer 2 July 1989.

Section III

Some Guidelines for Ignition

4. Beyond Vision

'*In dreams begins responsibility*'
Old play, Epigraph, Responsibilities, W.B. Yeats

There is no doubt that creating a powerful vision can act as a guiding light for an organization. A company's vision can become a catalyst and a guiding principle for everything that it does. However, belief in vision is a fairly new concept in business thinking. It comes out of knowing intuitively about things, trusting gut feeling and acknowledging that logic is not everything. The idea is simply that by envisioning the future you want, you can more easily achieve your goal. The tension between what is and what you'd like it to be is essential for mobilization of change.

The use of vision and visualization is better known in sport than in business, although it is rapidly becoming an acceptable business phenomenon. 'Research has shown that by picturing the successful completion of moves that they want to make, athletes can improve their performance, especially if the mental picture is accompanied by physical practice', write Michael Murphy and Rhea White in *The Psychic Side of Sports*. According to Murphy and White, Jack Nicklaus claims his best golf shots depend 10 per cent on his swing, 40 per cent on his set-up and 50 per cent on his mental picture. The British skater John Curry makes similar claims.

Now visualization has entered the business arena. Organizations are forming new images of their businesses and where they ought to be going. But vision is practical as well as mystical. It is easier to get from point A to point B if you know where point B is and how to recognize it when you've arrived. As David Campbell cautions: 'If you don't know where you're going, you'll probably end up somewhere else'.

Some examples of forceful, well-defined visions which both compel and challenge each member of the organization to pursue certain goals are as follows:

SAS's president, Jan Carlzon, envisions a market where 'the customer is always happy, costs are trimmed to the bone at the head office while more money is spent on service, businessmen are pampered without paying any extra on the standard planes, tourists fly for the price of second class rail travel, and profits flow in like clear water from the mountain stream'.

The vision of Apple Computer co-founder Steve Jobs was to bring technology to non-technical people. What distinguished Apple from the hundreds of other fledgling computer companies with dreams of becoming IBM's competitors was Job's insistence that his partner Wozniak should design features into the Apple with which techno-peasants like the rest of us could feel comfortable. Jobs had another vision, for Apple Computers to become a $10 billion dollar company by 1990.

Bill Gore, founder of W.L. Gore & Associates Inc., set out in 1958 to create a profitable company where he could recreate the sense of excitement and commitment he had felt as a member of a small task force in the research labs of E.I. Du Pont de Nemours. 'The task force', says Bill, 'was exciting, challenging and loads of fun. Besides, we worked like Trojans. I began to wonder why entire companies couldn't run in the same way.'

Effective visions are inspiring and like magnets they attract people and give them direction. The sharing of a vision provides a sense of purpose. The vision is especially powerful if it is based on a clearly stated set of values describing both the organization's mission and how it is to be achieved. The vision provides energy and direction. It is a magnet by which everyone aligns themselves toward a common purpose. A good example of vision is the US constitution and Bill of Rights. It is inspirational and offers a standard against which Americans can measure how well they are doing.

Creating a Vision

The first step is usually an ability to develop a mental image of a possible future organization – the vision is sometimes vague, sometimes clear as crystal. The main thing is that it should articulate an attractive yet credible future state for the organization. It paints a picture of an organization that is better in important ways than it is currently.

A vision is a target that inspires and attracts people. When John Kennedy shared his vision of putting a man on the moon and when Martin Luther King Jr declared 'I have a dream', they were focusing attention on the future, on something worth aiming for and something they passionately believed to be achievable. A vision helps to provide a link between where the organization is now and where it would like to be – it is always focused on the future.

Visionary leaders inspire their employees to high levels of achievement by showing them how their work contributes to important and worthwhile ends. Vision often works on an emotional level. History portrays figures like Kennedy and Churchill as possessing vision, and it is often written about as a very special inner resource. How then do people and organizational leaders create a vision? On closer examination of our client companies, it usually turns out that the vision did not in fact come from the chief executive personally, but from a number of other people. The chief executive may be the one who chooses the most compelling image from all those that were made available, and communicates it to the organization, but he/she is rarely the person who conceived it. The key skill for being able to create a vision seems to be the ability to listen, especially to those people who may have different images and scenarios of what could be in the future. Some companies we work with have established formal ways of listening for different ideas, others do it more informally. In creating a vision, our clients appear to focus their attention on the past of their organization and on the present state, and then build an alternative picture of what the future might be like.

The process of creating a vision frequently works like this. The first step is to reflect on experiences of the past within a particular company and also others in the same industry. This reflection on the past also focuses on different approaches, and our clients report that the best way of getting a feel for the past is by talking to people within the organization. This builds a picture of what mattered, what worked well and what did not. The stories, the mythology and the critical incidents reported by people who have been in the organization a long time are all relevant. They all help to form a picture of what the organization tried to do, how it achieved its objectives and what were the reasons for its success.

There is also a lot of data about the future all around us now. The present provides a rough guide to what resources will be available to form the future. Market research departments are often sitting on a lot of data about trends and other impending changes. Futurologists are constantly creating links between what is and what might be in the future. Government policies which will affect things for years to come are well publicized. All these provide early warning signals.

In looking ahead, clients report the need to focus on conditions that may prevail at some future point. Although it is not possible to predict with total accuracy and plan every detail, there are a number of clues. Currently much is written about future trends, whether they are to do with the changing structures of organizations, changing consumer needs, demographic data or opinion polls. All these various sources of information are useful when considering a possible future. There is plenty of information around – the real skill lies in interpreting the information and understanding how it may affect a particular organization.

Effective visions prepare for the future but honour the past. Ronald Reagan said in his inauguration speech as president: 'As you seek to change every procedure and job description to aid responsiveness, remember the bygone days when we whipped big competitors by being faster and fleeter of foot. You are safe in that you honour our most cherished traditions as you seek to break out of today's constraining bonds'. Reagan directed Congress towards being more responsive in the future while reminding them that they could learn from and retain the good things from bygone days.

The synthesis of a vision involves a great amount of judgement, intuition and creativity. It is the process of assembling and sorting out all the information, possible scenarios, forecasts and alternatives which will generate a vision. Most organizations we work with report that a clearly articulated vision of the future that is simple, easily understood, clearly desirable and generates energy is the most compelling. Decisions also need to be made about time frames, how far ahead it is possible to work, will the image be simple or complex, will it appear optimistic and will there be links to the past?

However, the creation of a desirable picture of the future by itself is not enough; the organization still needs to be able to translate this vision into action and to be able to move beyond vision.

BEYOND CREATING A VISION

How often do companies achieve their vision? What happens if there is a discrepancy between the ideal vision and the day to day work of the company?

Especially under pressure and at times of change and transition it is easier to become negative, to abandon the vision or ignore it. Senge and Kiefer believe that the tension between what is and what ought to be is actually healthy. 'The tension seeks resolution toward the vision. Each person is able to make decisions locally that are consistent with the whole, while not necessarily knowing the details of activities in other parts of the organization.'

The vision has to be powerful to attract in the first place. It has to be persistent, it has to be reinforced and re-energized constantly so that it becomes compelling. It has to be kept alive and this job often falls almost entirely on the chief executive.

Sir Colin Marshall, chief executive of British Airways, is a fine example. He is not only a visionary leader but his commitment to communicating his vision is legendary.

From our own experience of working with B.A. over the last six years, we can report on how this commitment works. Sir Colin Marshall keeps the vision alive in a number of ways that most people would expect, e.g. with videos and regular communication meetings. However, he also has the energy and commitment for much more than this. For instance he is often seen in the passenger terminals at Heathrow Airport at 7.00 a.m. talking with staff and passengers. British Airways launched a week-long management development programme as part of its culture change effort. The programme was for all managers and ran every week over a period of 18 months. Sir Colin attended each programme for approximately two hours over the 18-month period. He would arrive for an 8.00 a.m. meeting with the course participants, talk for a few minutes, bringing the managers up to date on most recent events in the airline, always emphasizing the vision, and then proceed to listen and answer questions for the rest of the time. Sir Colin did not miss more than a handful of these programmes and when he couldn't be there for the Friday morning, it was arranged for the course participants to meet him in the boardroom within the next few weeks. This commitment through words and presence has done more to help boost the culture change in B.A. than any other single event.

The chief executive not only attended as many management meetings as he could, he was also frequently present at the end of the day of a corporate event where up to 150 people from all over the airline, and worldwide, came together to talk about and renew their commitment to 'putting the customer first'. Sir Colin was often there for the last hour of the day, to talk to people, to listen, to seek views and answer questions. His role did not end there, because he would often spend some time afterwards informally with his staff. This is a fine example of the chief executive keeping the vision alive, by constantly articulating it, living it and getting personally involved in grounding the vision in everyday business, as well as listening to the staff's views.

In return, a few years later, B.A.'s 40,000 employees boosted the airline to enter the private sector with much confidence from the public. Sir Colin had re-organized B.A. by getting Ignition going and dramatically increased profits for B.A. with a powerful new vision. He made the company market-led and put the customer first.

Changing values, creating visions and new notions of things do not in themselves negotiate changes. Great business ideas and visions are not enough. The most important thing is the burning desire to realize and build the vision into reality. Don Burr, founder and former Chairman of People Express Inc., puts it very well when reviewing Waterman's recent book, *The Renewal Factor*. He says '(we) glide too easily over the backbreaking, heartrending task of implementing this vision. These ideas are a tough sell for the managers out there who have to deal with the runny noses and bloody arms of the workday world . . . (we) seem tentative and uneasy with the messy process of implementation'. He quotes his own experience with People Express and says, 'One whole organization structure was built around such directional or objective orientated concepts as commitment, teamwork and trust and we asked our people to adopt the company's objectives as their own. We asked them to work in both staff and line functions, to work in teams and share responsibility for implementing the objectives. We made sure, through profit-sharing and stock ownership, among other community programmes, that they would think of the airline as their own, and that they would share in its success. We committed resources to teaching, training, coaching and helping people better understand the direction and what was necessary to get there'.

He continues, 'even if over time, you get widespread agreement on objectives, as we did, you still have to design a powerful, self-reinforcing process to get consistent creative implementation.'

A lot has been written about the need for vision to be inspiring, elegant, simple, powerful and persuasive, but the danger is that people will quickly dismiss vision as utterly romantic and unrealistic; vision requires heroic commitment, or it is easily lost in the strong forces of bureaucracy.

A vision needs three key elements; focus, flexibility and persistence. It needs to be specific, so that it can give a sharp focus and keep the organization focused on its purpose, but at the same time it needs to be general, so that people in the organization can be bold enough to take initiatives in the changing environment. There is an urgent need to keep the focus sharp on whatever it is that an organization is trying to achieve. Taking too long over it will result in missed opportunities and loss of competitive edge. Riccardo Berla, chairman of Olivetti in the UK, said, 'Product development (in Olivetti) used to take two years or so. Today Bellini produces mass design in two months'. That is the new, focused way of doing things.

Secondly, day to day flexibility and innovation by everyone can only occur if the vision is clear, unmistakable, inspiring and exciting. Directing organizational energy towards quick response and fast initiative taking needs a soaring purpose – a vision and a set of values that are responsive to today's needs and also starting to provide answers to tomorrow's needs.

Bennis and Nanus described leaders that they studied as 'creating dangerously' and as 'creating the basic metabolism of their organization'. Managers and leaders must continue to create new worlds, and then destroy them, and then create afresh. Such brave acts of creation must begin with a vision that not only inspires and challenges, but at the same time provokes confidence, so that even in the turbulent times of change, it can still encourage people to take the day to day risks involved in testing, adapting and extending the vision.

While a vision must provide stability, it must also inspire confidence to induce constant risk taking in pursuit of its execution, but must not be constrained by yesterday's success patterns. Constant and active listening to the customer and the competitor, promoting innovation, flatter organizational structures and keeping close to the market all encourage flexibility and initiative taking which will, over a period of time, change the operational definition of the vision at the margin and may even eventually change it dramatically. Vision needs this kind of flexibility.

Finally it must be persistent. If organizations are to get beyond just creating a vision, then they need follow–through, to get back to it again and again in everything they do.

The speed of response that is expected from an organization today can only occur if people within it have a clear understanding of what it is trying to achieve. But vision on its own is not enough. If creating and proclaiming the vision is over-used in the hope that this alone will guide the organization, there is a danger that it may stifle innovation and reduce creativity. It may prevent organizations benefiting from productive departures from a major plan that could produce entirely new products or strategies. There needs to be a clear vision and a plan for how to get there and there needs to be an acknowledgement that the plan may be departed from or amended.

Vision alone is not enough, shared understanding is the next step as well as techniques and specialities. Only a combination of these will help to go beyond vision.

ALIGNMENT OR GETTING COMMITMENT

Creating a vision is the first job. Next comes getting other people in the organization to share the vision and to own it. Peter Senge and Charles Kiefer have studied both vision and that special blend of high performance and workability called alignment. When alignment exists, there is a fit between the company's goals and the individual's goals. Senge and Kiefer call organizations that achieve this state metanoic, a Greek word used by the early Christians, meaning re-awakening of vision and intuition.

The Metanoic Organization
Senge and Kiefer explain the key elements of metanoic organizations by considering what is required to mould an Olympic crew from a group of talented rowers. First, the crew need to commit themselves to being champions. Olympic performance does not come from merely wanting to win the next race, but from striving to win the Olympics. To excel truly, the team must have a vision that is long-term and sufficiently challenging to develop peak performance over an extended period of time.

But vision alone is not enough. The individual commitment and talent needs to be translated into collective accomplishment and this requires alignment of all the individual energies. Rowing together represents a whole new dimension. Many people find it difficult and frustrating, but when a team starts to work together effectively, something exciting and different happens. Each individual begins to perceive a totally new sensation as eight blades strike the water in unison. There comes a unique rush of energy with the recognition of what the team can accomplish. When this condition of alignment is allowed to develop, individuals transcend their roles as separate team members to experience themselves as the entire team during periods of exceptional performance.

Vision and alignment are still insufficient. If we take the most committed aligned rowers and put them in a leaky boat, they won't win many races. A poorly designed boat will easily thwart the efforts of the best crew. Finally, the team need an environment that continually allows talents to develop. It must commit itself to a training discipline that allows each individual's capabilities to develop to the fullest.

Senge and Kiefer use the crew analogy to point to four unique elements underlying metanoic organizations:

1. Vision

2. Alignment

3. Structural integrity

4. Personal mastery

Such organizations invariably have a clear sense of a shared vision. They develop individual talent and evolve organization structure and policy to translate individual energies efficiently into collective action.

Alignment

Effective leaders catalyse alignment through sharing their vision and enabling others to do likewise. Through individuals communicating their personal visions, recognition of a common underlying purpose emerges. With this recognition, individuals see that by fully expressing their own purpose and power they naturally further the achievement of the organization's purpose.

In one of our client companies where a comprehensive culture change programme was under way, an interesting and different method of alignment was used. The top team went away for a weekend to create a vision for the organization and write a mission statement. This was to be used as a starting point on one of the culture change programmes for the participants to plan how they could contribute to achieving the company's mission. However, the top team emerged from their weekend hideout dissatisfied with their version of the vision and the mission statement. They charged the consultants responsible for the training programme to invite participants to create their own vision for the organization and draft a mission statement. The top 1,000 managers were to attend this programme. Each individual was invited to create and generate a vision of the organization. In small teams of up to seven people, each individual shared his/her vision with members of the team. They pulled together the key themes and produced a team vision. The teams were encouraged to present their vision of the organization creatively and not necessarily in written form. Some teams used drama, others songs, pictures, mime, sculpture, poetry and many other creative methods. What emerged from this exercise was that although individuals expressed their personal visions, there were many common underlying themes. Thus when the participants were further invited to translate the vision into a mission statement, again common themes emerged. The process of producing a personal vision and then a team vision and translating this into a mission statement helped the alignment process. The top team then took away these hundreds of mission statements and finally produced a corporate mission statement which appeared to have integrated the most common themes. The whole process was very visible: people felt involved in giving the company direction and were rewarded by having their ideas integrated into the final version of the corporate mission.

Most commonly, the top team or the leader generates the vision and the mission statement and then proceeds to the difficult and time-consuming task of getting organization alignment. Getting people to 'buy in' to something to which they have not contributed generally takes longer.

In order to move beyond creating a vision to the translation of individual commitment and energy into collective action requires the alignment of the individuals. People have to be able to see how their personal contribution will help to achieve the organization's goals. Individuals need to be able to move beyond their own specific goals if they are to help make the vision a reality.

Mission Statements or Corporate Credos

For many companies, the late 80s and early 90s have been a time when they have needed to refocus their corporate energies. One way of moving beyond vision and refocusing energies is generating a 'mission statement'. Typically, a mission statement is a charter that defines the basic business in which the organization will engage, the type of product it will make or the services it will provide, the markets it will serve, and perhaps how the company will conduct its affairs; in other words, its purpose. A good mission statement can be used to establish a firm foundation for guiding the company.

Company staff are usually the main audience for a mission statement. Often the statement helps to increase commitment further. The act of devising a mission statement often forces management to take a hard look at external threats and opportunities as well as internal strengths and weaknesses. A mission statement can also provide a frame of reference for the entire planning effort and a set of standards for new products, and it can help a company determine its proper market niche.

Organizations use many different ways of generating mission statements. Here are some of the key principles that are frequently used:

- The first step is often a SWOT analysis, i.e. identifying the internal strengths and weaknesses of the organization as well as doing an analysis of the opportunities and threats confronting the organization. The group developing the mission statement will often ask the following questions: What have we been doing? What do we want to change? However, the mission statement must help to set the future direction of the company. The statement will be useless if it is simply a rationalization of what the company has been doing.

- Different companies choose different criteria for defining the business. It depends on what is appropriate for the particular company. The following alternatives are most commonly used: by the products the company produces; by unique resources that the company possesses; by a particular strength that the company has; by unique financial measures or by needs that are met.

- Our clients often try to strike a balance between too wide and too narrow a definition of the business. Too wide a definition can leave the organization with no real direction, while too narrow a statement can block management from seeing environmental changes, opportunities and threats.

- Those clients who have developed mission statements and are using them successfully usually ensure that senior management can and will dedicate itself to the statement. This means that before the mission statement is published, all those who will be affected by it in a significant way are asked to grasp its implications and be able to live with the consequences. That means being able to accept the process of change. Some mission statements imply a totally new direction for the company, while others place limits on change.

- The chief executive who is involved in devising the mission statement will often be more comfortable with the end product. This raises a practical problem, i.e. if up to 20 managers have to devise a mission statement jointly, it can be a long unwieldy process. However, if the mission statement is the product of the chief executive alone, then it is likely to be that individual's mission statement, not necessarily the company's.

- The golden rule is to keep the mission statement short and to the point. As Judith Katz Geschwin, a senior vice-president of American Express's Travel Related Services Company recommends, 'Tell the world in 25 words or less who you are and what you want to become'.

We have found that when our clients are serious about moving beyond vision, the next step after creating a vision is often to ground that vision in a mission statement which helps different parts of the organization to set their goals and objectives.

VISIONARY LEADERSHIP

The late 80s and early 90s brought turbulence to the business world. The general feeling amongst organizations seemed to be 'we need to do something new and significantly different'. Doing more of the same was only delivering marginal returns. There seemed to be a need for a more substantial change. The change had to help organizations make quantum leaps and so it had to be visionary. An effective vision provides guidance and direction.

In the past few years, much has been written about the need for visionary leadership. This does not mean that rational, analytical skills are no longer required, but there is a need for both intuition and rational skills. Today's visionary leaders have the job of seeing that a vision is created and then enlisting support for it both inside and outside the organization. Visionary leaders like Sir Colin Marshall appear to have three major responsibilities:

1. They are the safekeepers of the company's vision.

2. They enlist support both inside and particularly from outside the organization.

3. They anticipate and help to manage the future.

From working with a number of emerging visionary leaders, we have perceived that it is not always necessary for these leaders to create the vision themselves; they appear to make sure that a vision, and a mission describing how to achieve the vision, are formulated. They inspire and legitimize the creation of a shared and compelling vision. Once the vision has been created, the visionary leader is then responsible for articulating and communicating this vision, for keeping it alive and updated and enlisting support from others. The leaders themselves have to understand and practise the core values articulated in the vision, because their responsibility as a role-model starts immediately and seems to be constantly in the spotlight.

In our experience, visionary leaders quickly move beyond creating a vision by enlisting support both from inside and particularly from the stakeholders. Customers, staff, suppliers, shareholders, unions, governments and communities all have expectations that need to be met. The backing of these major stakeholders is required if an organization is to realize its vision. Visionary leaders mobilize the energy and commitment necessary to get the process of implementation started. Lord King and Sir Colin Marshall put together a 'road show' in which they told the public about their plans for when B.A. had been privatized and answered questions from would-be shareholders. This helped to enlist suport from their major stakeholders to help them move beyond the vision of being a privatized organization. Inevitably, articulating vision will also bring challenges and criticism. Visionary leaders will persist in the face of resistance and scepticism.

The third responsibility of a visionary leader is to be able to anticipate the future and help to manage it. Focusing attention on the future provides the necessary awareness to remain responsive to changes in market trends and demands. Sir John Harvey-Jones was talking about 'Europe' in 1972, 20 years before the 1992 deregulation would come into effect. This is a good example of anticipating and helping to manage the future.

Vision lives in the intensity of the leader, an intensity that itself draws in others. The key purpose of a vision is to provide the bedrock upon which constant change can take place. It is all too easy for even the most compelling vision to become static, getting in the way of the very change it is meant to induce. Despite everything, the vision still has a good chance of getting rusty. It is the job of the visionary leader to keep it fresh and live. 'The very essence of Leadership is (that) you have to have a vision. It's got to be a vision you articulate clearly and forcefully on every occasion. You can't blow an uncertain trumpet'. (Father Theodore Hesburgh, former president, Notre Dame University).

Great leadership demands the ability to create and communicate a vision that points the way for others. The power of such a vision stems directly from its use as a vehicle for elucidating an underlying, and often intangible, organizational purpose. A workable, captivating vision serves both as a vehicle for people to discover an underlying purpose and as a magnet around which they can align.

Leadership requires a balance between intuition and rational analysis. There are no rules for creating a vision that inspires people – visioning is a deeply intuitive process. As well as intuition leaders must have the ability to examine and clarify complex organizational dynamics and analyse often ill-defined issues. Great leaders develop a unique interplay between intuition and reason. They use intuition to guide their analysis and they continually subject their intuitive insights to rational examination.

Bennis and Nanus' *Leaders* summarizes it well: 'Visionary Leaders require foresight, so they can judge how the vision fits into the way the environment of the organization may evolve: hindsight, so that the vision does not violate the traditions and culture of the organization; a world view, within which to interpret the impact of possible new developments and trends; depth perception, so that the whole picture can be seen in appropriate detail and perspective; peripheral vision, so that the possible response of competitors and other stakeholders to the new direction can be comprehended: and a process of revision, so that all visions previously synthesised are constantly reviewed as the environment changes.'

FOLLOW-THROUGH

New Jersey based Johnson & Johnson is the largest health care product company in the USA. J & J's statement of values called simply 'our credo' is a 295-word document in which the corporation puts great stock. Job applicants are told about it. All new employees get a copy and an explanation. According to the company, the credo played an important role in the 1982 Tylenol crisis, in which seven people in the Chicago area died after taking Extra Strength Tylenol contaminated with cyanide. When the news bulletins appeared, J & J managers verified the reports and promptly ordered every package, everywhere, off the shelves and back to the company. Though officials were fairly certain that the deaths were caused by foul play within the Chicago area only, no one questioned the necessity of the cost of the recall. It was simply the thing to be done. It was the only action possible that was entirely consistent with the first and fourteenth sentences of the credo:

We believe our first responsibility is to the doctors, nurses and patients, to mothers and all others who use our products and services.
We are responsible to the communities in which we live and work, and the world community as well.

The Tylenol crisis had all the makings of a total disaster, that could have brought lasting damage to the credibility of the company and its products. J & J's unhesitating willingness to follow through from their stated credo and to take a drastic short-term financial loss amounted to a masterpiece of long-range thinking, not to mention public relations. The display of corporate responsibility and concern was all the more dramatic when contrasted with the familiar evasive cynicism with which so many companies respond to negative news about their products. J & J emerged from the Tylenol scare smelling like a rose. If the company had not backed up its publicly stated credo, it could easily have backfired with serious loss of market share.

We wrote part of this book while on a sabbatical, in a rented house in the Utah Rockies. The place was a small ski resort, fairly isolated and a good 45 minutes drive from the nearest city. A local pizza place advertised its services and boasted a large clientele to whom it could deliver their choice of pizza within ten minutes of ordering. Their published credo was 'to know our customers well and deliver their choice of pizza within ten minutes.' The first time we used this service, the person taking our order was careful to take our name, address and telephone number and the required pizza was delivered to us fast. A few weeks later, we rang again to order another pizza dinner. As soon as we gave our name on the telephone, the person at the other end, without any hesitation said 'oh yes, and the address is 2750 Holiday Ranch, Loop Road etc. what would you like to order this evening?' We were impressed with her knowledge and ability to retrieve the necessary data (i.e. the address) while we were still talking on the telephone. We placed our order and we made some notes to include this as a good example of a published credo at work. Unfortunately, the service went no further; the company took one and a half hours to deliver our pizza, with no explanation or apology. The next time we ordered (giving them the benefit of the doubt), the same thing happened. Their telephone answering service was good at following through and letting the customers know that the pizza company knew them and valued them enough to hold their names and addresses in their data base; but their delivery service could not keep the promise of delivering within ten minutes, thus losing the organization credibility and probably other customers as well as ourselves.

In our experience, successful companies develop a vision, and then live it vigorously. Sometimes vision and values are proclaimed, but not fulfilled. Posters and wallet-sized cards are printed, but no one 'lives' them. To turn vision into a beacon, leaders at all levels must behave consistently with the vision at all times. They live a vision, not just a formal declaration. Effective visions are made of stuff that can be used on a moment to moment, day to day basis.

3i, probably the world's largest source of private capital, with investments in 4,500 companies, has invested some £10 billion over the past decade. It has been involved in 2,000 start-ups and 100 management buyouts. One figure that it watches is its failure rate. Recently, 200 ventures backed by 3i went to the wall. Does that make 3i edge further towards no risk? The answer is, no, it doesn't. 'If none of them were a failure', said Foulds, the chief executive, 'that would be a clear sign we were not investing enough. We cannot be in the risk business without failures, and it is a golden rule that we never witch hunt over an investment that went wrong.' Moving beyond vision means having the courage to follow through with the proclaimed values.

IMPLEMENTING VISION

We have found that organizations that are good at moving beyond vision start the implementation process early. Creating the vision is considered only as the first step. Communicating the vision and enlisting support for it are on-going activities. In these organizations the planning for implementation starts early.

PLAN-DO CYCLES

The importance of alternating planning and implementing in short 'plan-do' cycles was noted in *Superteams*.

Essentially this means getting away from the linear and traditionally used process of planning an event, intervention, product etc. from beginning to end before the implementation process starts. This causes difficulty in a number of ways, especially in a rapidly changing business environment. By the time the planning has been completed, the product may already be obsolete. Competitors will have brought something new onto the market. We advocate shorter cycles, i.e. planning just enough to get things going but starting to implement in parallel or at least shortly afterwards; coming back and planning a little more but continuing the parallel implementation. This has a number of positive results:

- Implementation starts early so there is less chance of the whole plan being rejected.

- There is immediate feedback from the market-place or the organization as to the results of change which can help in the next planning stage.

- There is an opportunity to test and then adapt.

- Changing market and environment factors can be taken into account.

- It provides the flexibility that is needed in a rapidly changing world.

We need to move away from lengthy, long-term planning to multiple, short plan-do cycles. Each plan-do cycle is like a quick in and out, ground-level excursion into unknown territory. Each cycle produces more data which enables the planner to predict and plan further ahead than they could before. The pay-offs from early excursions are great so that relatively quickly it is possible to have a realistic plan or map of most of the territory, with some pretty clear indicators of the paths to be taken to the other side.

One of the biggest barriers to implementing Ignition and moving beyond creating a vision is the attitude that organizations have towards planning. Too much time and energy is devoted to trying to predict the unpredictable in an effort to reduce risk, uncertainty and ambiguity. This often results in highly complex and sophisticated plans which in fact induce rigidity and inhibit innovation. The traditional ways in which planning is done has the effect of extending lead time and reducing quality and productivity. It also often makes it difficult to experience those successes that are so important in maintaining commitment, high energy levels and the willingness to pursue further activities and overcome problems.

Increasingly, organizations are finding different ways of working useful in their attempt to move beyond vision and in dealing with uncertain situations and a constantly changing market place.

PLANNING

Recent work with several different companies has convinced us that the way managers and technical specialists think about planning can be a major block to moving beyond vision. We often use a simple exercise on training programmes where a group of people are given a project and asked to devise the most efficient way of doing it. A number of key things happen:

- Almost always a separate unit of planners is set up and those responsible for implementation are largely excluded from the planning process.

- The planners deliver the results of the planning process to the implementing group, telling them what has to be done, dictating time-scales and setting out a plan of how it is to be done. This is only done after the detailed plan is completed.

- The 'doing' phase of the project is always a separate activity that follows after the detailed planning phase, as in a relay race.

- Before the implementers can do anything, they often have a communication problem, because the key elements of the plan are expressed in planners' jargon.

- A lot of time is spent arguing on exactly how long each of the activities is going to take and in what order they should be done.

- The activities in the implementation phase are ordered in a linear fashion, one activity only starting after the previous one has been completed (relay race).

Managers can often be heard saying things like: 'We missed the boat', 'The project was delivered late and over budget' and so on. The common thread running through all these situations is that 'things haven't gone according to plan'. Planning, which is a very persuasive form of thinking, cannot by definition deal with ambiguous, uncertain and complex problems that organizations face today, especially during times of rapid change.

PARALLEL PLAN-DO

In reality, planning and doing often have to happen in parallel and in many uncertain situations doing can precede planning. Doing, linked to reflection and observation, is a more potent method of reducing uncertainty than planning. It is not possible to plan the unknown. Doing is quicker, it engages reality directly and above all it provides feedback from the unknown. The feedback dispels more ambiguity than any amount of planning can and provides vital experience for planning the next stage. We advocate multiple, short plan-do cycles to help move beyond vision. Each cycle maps a little more of the unknown territory. Each cycle produces more data which enables us to plan a little further ahead. The pay-offs in the short term also help to keep the motivation up and reward the efforts to date, thus reinforcing the vision and providing future direction.

Planners and Doers need to do it Together

In implementing change and moving beyond vision, specialists often pass on instructions to another group who have to make it happen. Planners and doers need to be brought together early. All those who contribute to the realization of a concept need to be brought in quickly. Creating a vision and a mission statement may well be the job of a small group of people, but moving beyond vision requires everyone in the organization. This energy needs to be mobilized early if the doers are to be committed to the planners' concepts.

Planning the What and Planning the How

Planning the 'what' involves identifying the goals and the means for achieving them. Planning the 'how' involves planning the social processes of how to communicate the 'what' to the doers, how to get the implementers' acceptance and commitment to the plan and how to deal with situations where the planning and the doing don't match. When planning, there needs to be an equal balance of emphasis on 'planning the what' and 'planning the how'. Implementers can contribute their expertise to planning the 'what' and the 'how', thus short-circuiting the later problems of how to communicate, get acceptance, commitment and how to deal with uncertainties.

Often a lot of energy is put into trying to map out the whole implementation process in detail. The process being used is to plan the whole and then do the whole. In moving beyond vision, and keeping it flexible, only the broad activities and milestones and how to get people involved need to be planned. The energy needs to be focused on moving forward fast. Frequent plan–do cycles within this broad framework of parallel activities will help to get implementation started.

Tidy/Messiness

In moving beyond vision, there is often a tendency to do things in a tidy, structured, step by step fashion. In reality, the process is messy and we need to be able to live with messiness. Short plan–do cycles are essentially messy. In implementing change, it is possible at times to make big leaps with only a small amount of effort and at other times, given the reality, it is best to move back a little or even return to the starting point.

Pitfalls

Stanley M. Davis has catalogued a number of problems and pitfalls that can sabotage the effort to capture an organization's mission, communicate it and then implement it. Four of the key pitfalls are:

1. *Lip-service:* if people in the organization talk about the company's mission, but nobody actually does anything different.

2. *Cynicism:* this is the most common pitfall. What the people at the top actually do is totally at odds with the vision and the espoused mission, and everyone knows it.

3. *The Non-Event:* corporate events with a lot of razzamataz, videos, posters, memos etc. announce that the company is going to pay attention to its mission and to its culture and make sure that the vision is identified and communicated. Then, nothing. Senior managers don't see much point in it all. Other more immediate needs arise or there is a crisis and the whole thing gets put on the 'one of these days' list.

4. *Blandness:* all the work is wasted if the end-product is so watered down that it becomes banal. Today everyone seems to think that the word 'excellence' must be part of the vision or else it won't be right. The genuine vision and the credo need to be so specific to a particular company, that they would probably be almost useless to another organization.

While creating a vision can be done by a small group of people, communicating it can be managed by the communications division or the public relations experts, when it comes to moving beyond that stage, the whole organization has to be mobilized. That is where the next challenge lies. Beyond vision lies the real challenge of implementation.

Flashpoints

BEYOND VISION

Effective visions are inspiring and act like a magnet. They are there to attract people and give them direction and energy. Sharing a vision provides a sense of direction for the organization.

Creating a Vision
- Focus attention on the past, on the present and develop a mental picture of what the future might be like.

  Past: reflect on the past; on the history; on the traditions. Build a picture of what mattered; what worked well and what didn't.

  Present: focus on what is available e.g. resources.

  Future: examine the conditions that may prevail. Interpret the available information.

- Creating a vision requires a synthesis of the past, present and future. It requires the use of judgement, intuition and creativity.

Beyond creating a Vision
- Focus: keep it sharp and specific.

- Flexible: keep it general, so that there is room for creativity, initiative and change of direction when needed.

- Follow-Through: the vision needs to be kept alive, reinforced, re-energized and persistent.

Alignment or Getting Commitment
- The first task is to create a vision. The next most important task is to share the vision and get other people to own it.

- To get alignment, help individuals to understand how their personal contribution will help to achieve the organizational goal.

Mission Statements

A mission statement defines the basic business i.e. its purpose. Establishing a mission statement helps to keep the vision in focus and furthers commitment.

In preparing a mission statement, examine:

- External threats and opportunities.

- Internal strengths and weaknesses.

- Criteria for defining the business.

- The balance between too narrow and too wide a definition.

- Keep it brief – 25 words or less.

- Whether or not senior management can dedicate themselves to the contents of the mission statement.

Visionary Leadership

Visionary leaders have three main responsibilities in helping organizations to move beyond vision:

- They are the safekeepers of the company's vision.

- They enlist support from both inside and outside the organization.

- They anticipate and help to manage the future.

Follow-Through

- Back up the publicly stated credo with appropriate actions.

- Live the vision vigorously.

- Don't just have a formal declaration of the vision: model behaviour that is consistent with the declared vision.

Implementing Vision
- Plan for implementation early.

- Get away from the traditional, linear planning process. Use short plan-do cycles. Each cycle provides feedback and data which can be used to predict the future.

- Planning and doing need to start in parallel.

- Plan the broad activities and set milestones, instead of planning for every detail.

- Doing is more productive than planning what is unpredictable.

- Planners and doers need to work together from an early stage.

- Plan both what has to be done and how it will be done.

- Implementing vision is an untidy, messy process.

Pitfalls
In moving beyond vision, there are some pitfalls that need to be watched:

- Paying lip-service rather than doing.

- Cynicism – saying one thing and doing another.

- A lot of razzamataz in communicating the vision, followed by no action.

- Turning vision into an elegant piece of writing, but then nothing happens.

- Creating a bland, generalized vision which is not specific to the company.

REFERENCES

- Murphy, M. and White, R. (1978) *The Psychic Side of Sports*, Wokingham: Addison-Wesley.

- Campbell, D. (1974) *If you don't know where you're going you'll probably end up somewhere else*, Argus Communication.

- *International Management.* December 1982.

- Levering, R., Moskowitz, M. and Katz, M. (1984) *The 100 Best companies to work for in America*, Wokingham: Addison-Wesley.

- *'The Un-Manager'*, Inc. August 1982.

- Senge, P. and Kiefer, C. *'Metanoic Organizations: New Experiments on Organizational Design'*, (an unpublished paper).

- Time, May 1987.

- Burr, D. Reviews Waterman's recent book *The Renewal Facter*, Inc Feb 1988.

- Bennis, W. (1984) *'The Four Competencies of Leadership'*, Training and Development Journal August 1984.

- Bennis, W. and Nanus, B. (1985) *Leaders*, London: Harper and Row Ltd.

- Davis, S.M. (1984) *Managing Corporate Culture*, 1984 Bollinger.

- Pilditch, J. (1987) *Winning Ways*, London: Harper and Row Ltd.

- Hastings, C., Bixby, P., Chaudhry-Lawton, R. (1986) *Superteams*, London: Fontana.

- Zemke, R. '*Stalking the Elusive Corporate Credo*', Training June 1985 Lakewood Publications Inc.

- Naisbitt, J. and Aburdene, P. (1985) *Re-inventing the Corporation*, New York: Warner Books.

5. Start Somewhere

'A good plan violently executed right now is far better than a perfect plan executed next week.'
General George Patton

Too many change initiatives are strangled by over-analysis or fear of the likely consequences. This chapter is about people and groups who have the ability to overcome this. They share the desire to get things moving and take risks where necessary. There is never a right time to get Ignition started, but here are some strategies which might be useful.

Talk About It

When Ed Carlson took over the troubled United Airlines, it was heavily bureaucratic and simply did not work. Carlson knew he had to motivate everyone right down to the baggage handlers, so he started travelling and talking to his staff. He logged 186,000 miles touring United facilities in his first year. At each stop, Carlson told his people what was going on in United management and encouraged them to do what they thought was best for the company within the scope of their own jobs.

Managers and other people who have been central to getting the change process started in their organizations report that it is important to talk about change, all of it or a small part of it, how it will affect people, its advantages and disadvantages, what it will look like, how other people or outsiders might see it and so on. Talking about the change seems to help people to become familiar with it, to keep it alive and get used to it. Not talking about it does not make the change go away. Where possible, it is important to reduce secretiveness and avoid giving people surprises that may be construed as nasty. Talking about it helps get Ignition going by ensuring that the particular change is always in people's minds. It increases a sense of security if future plans are known in advance, thus making it possible in turn for those people below to be able to make their plans and set their goals.

It may not always be possible to talk about change in a positive way. That does not really matter; being able to talk about the fears, the confusion and uncertainties, will help to get things started. The effect is that of clarifying and acknowledging things for the change initiator and perhaps more importantly for the other people who cannot or will not articulate what they may be thinking, feeling or fearing.

Talking about the change can have other effects too. It can, for example, generate excitement and curiosity in others. As word travels, the more people get to hear of the change and become familiar with the idea. When they formally hear about it, it is no longer a surprise; it is something they have come to expect. It also starts the process of getting commitment. Some people will be allies straight away, while others may want to sit on the fence for a while and there will always be some people who resist the change. At least getting the early supporters on board helps to increase momentum and gets more people thinking about and discussing the change. An instance comes to mind, where a close friend announced at a party that she had an ambition to gather a group of people who would be willing to climb Mount Kilimanjaro in Africa with her. Once she got hold of the idea and had seen a glimmer of interest in a number of other people, Mount Kilimanjaro, climbing and expeditions seemed to enter the conversation at every possible opportunity. It was impossible to ignore the message. By the end of the evening, a number of people were ready to sign up for the expedition and a few more wanted to explore the idea further.

Talking about the change can work rather like a self-fulfilling prophecy. The more people talk about it, the more they come to expect it. The more attention and time gets focused on the issue, the sooner some action starts, directed very much at making sure the change does happen. 1992 is clearly an important date in the European calendar. From this year far more free trade between the European countries will be possible. Clearly it poses both opportunities and threats for all British and European businesses. Some companies started talking about this change and the effect of it 20 years ago, others are only just becoming aware of it. Judging by the number of seminars taking place, advertisements placed by the Department of Trade on radio, television, newspapers and billboards, it appears that talking about 1992 is helping the British public to understand the implications of this change. The discussion is helping people to understand that it will happen and that it will affect them; that now is the time to plan for the consequences and set the scene so that businesses are in a position to take advantage of the opportunities that lie ahead as well as make plans for dealing with the threats.

When Carlzon took over SAS and Sir Colin Marshall took over B.A., both men spent much of their time talking to staff, customers and competitors about things to come and their ideas to rejuvenate the two airlines. It helped to sow the seeds and get action started for both these massive Ignition projects. A more recent example of a campaign both in the USA and the UK, to help educate people about the Aids virus, started similarly. Advertisements, helplines, leaflets, seminars and many other activities were designed by the health authorities to educate people, to bring the subject to the public's attention by talking about it and signalling the consequences of people not changing their sexual habits.

DON'T WORRY ABOUT IT BEING PERFECT FIRST TIME ROUND

Waiting until it is absolutely right, with all the i's dotted and the t's crossed, might cost an organization the competitive edge. There is a need to get comfortable with trying it out even if it's not perfect. Aiming for excellence is a fine ambition, but 70 per cent might be enough to get started. If organizations continue to want to achieve the last 30 per cent, they may well miss the race or the opportunity. Ideally it would be good to feel that everybody in the organization was planning the forward direction absolutely correctly, but in reality this is an impossible aim. It is far more important to get started and to be moving forward in roughly the right direction than to be stuck still without the business going anywhere. The process of deciding the direction of change is the opportunity to get the involvement and commitment of others, which actually forms the motivation and helps to get the change implemented. Determination alone is not enough, however; it seems easier to alter direction on the move than when an organization is static.

Peters and Waterman in their book *In Search of Excellence*, report that for one of the 3M vice-presidents the following is enough: 'We consider a coherent sentence to be an acceptable first draft for a new product plan'. Another example reported by Philip Goldberg in his book *The Intuitive Edge*, illustrates how James Couzens followed his intuition even though things did not look perfect. One night in 1893 James Couzens, a humble clerk in a Detroit coal company, saw someone rolling down a street in a noisy contraption that had been put together in a tool house from salvaged parts and bicycle wheels. As bystanders laughed, Couzens sensed that the bizarre vehicle and the eccentric behind the wheel represented more than entertainment. He took the thousand dollars he had saved and made a down payment on stock in the inventor's company. He also made a commitment to raise another $9,000 to bring his investment up to a hundred shares. In 1919, Couzens sold his stock in Henry Ford's company for $35 million.

Whether it is an idea or a product, it is essential to get implementation started from day one. Testing the idea or the product provides feedback which can help to modify the product as necessary. Getting a pilot scheme started is invaluable both for the individual initiating the change and for the Ignition process. While it provides feedback which helps to iron out the problems, it also gives the rest of the organization an opportunity to see the change in action. It brings the change alive and makes it a reality much faster and much sooner than the implementation of the whole detailed plan.

GIVE IT A NAME OR A SYMBOL

A name or a symbol or something that people can relate to will often help to get the change started. If a name or a symbol can be used when referring to the change project, it gives the organization a very strong signal that this entity exists. It makes it more real and helps to move Ignition forward. Names and symbols also help people involved in the change to keep focused, while helping to clarify the intent, simplify it and capture people's imagination. For example, Taylor Woodrow's logo of a team of men all pulling in the same direction is a powerful symbol of teamwork.

Within a much larger culture change effort at British Airways, a small group of line managers were selected for an intensive training programme. These line managers were trained so that they could work as fellow trainers with the external consultants on a one week residential programme called 'Managing People First'. This programme was conducted for 1,000 managers over a period of two years. The additional objective of training the line managers as trainers was that they would act as torch-bearers for the large culture change programme. They were called upon to be change agents and to model behaviours appropriate to the new culture. The slogan accompanying the symbol used for the programme was a quote from the Greek philosopher Archimedes: 'Give me a lever and a place to stand and I will move the world'.

HAVE YOU TALKED TO THEM?

It is often difficult to know exactly where to start from, especially if the change is big and complex. Often a good place is to start talking to the people who will be affected by the change. Sometimes, when planning the change, organizations can get stuck at a certain point, because the assumption is that, for example, the unions will not agree. When we have questioned people closely, we have often found that nobody has actually talked to the unions so far. Some typical questions worth asking are: How about the customers, have they been consulted or their views sought? Do the engineers know they have to create something different? Does the marketing department know of the intentions? Do the premises people know of the requirements? Does the personnel department know about the extra people required for the project? Does the legal department know of the plans? Are they checking the legalities? Does the local authority know about the building plans? They all point in the same direction i.e. talk to people, especially those who will be involved with the change, early.

MOBILIZE THE NETWORKS

In getting started, help is often needed from other people, whether it is from the formal network or the informal network. Networks can stretch horizontally as well as vertically, inside as well as outside the organization. The quicker they are brought into the picture, the easier their involvement and therefore the chances of success and commitment are increased. We have noticed that those people who use networks effectively have a tendency to let both the internal and the external network know of their intentions early. Often this is the time when personal favours and support are called in. Mobilizing the personal network of the change agent is often helpful in breaking down ineffective organizational barriers and creating pockets of positive change agents in different parts of the organization. Other change writers have borrowed the scientific term of 'creating a critical mass' to gain momentum for the change effort. One step towards this is to identify and tap into the appropriate network.

Experience in organizational change has shown that in addition to developing a plan for carrying out the change, it is equally important to determine who in the organization must be commited to the change and to carry it out, if the change is actually to take place. Traditionally, this is seen as a political stance, e.g. 'We've got to get a few people on board', 'get the chief executive's approval', 'get the union leadership to agree' or 'have the majority of the engineers going along'. We suggest that in addition to 'who needs to be committed', there is also a need to identify who might provide the resources or be able to develop this idea further, and who might act as the torch-bearer for this change. These people can often be identified and brought on board by mobilizing the informal network.

Networks are useful in many different ways. They may be able to help with tangible resources like spare money, personnel or equipment. However, the intangibles are extremely important too, for example psychological support, advice, acting as a sounding board or helping to open doors. Often in order to accelerate Ignition, the pieces of the jigsaw need to be ready well in advance. It may be too late to wait and collect the pieces when they are needed. The most common tangible pieces that are needed in times of change are to secure people, money, materials, time and information. In order to be sure of these, the networks need to be mobilized early and a lot of groundwork will also be necessary, in order to mobilize the intangible resources – by which we mean the confidence, trust, ideas and active support from others inside and outside the organization.

Rosabeth Moss Kanter, in her study of successful entrepreneurs, *The Change Masters*, found that these people were excellent at systematically building up their connections inside and outside the organization. The result was that they always had access to a network of people who could help. This was one of the secrets behind their ability to get things done where others failed. According to John Newhouse, the Lockheed Corporation began its programme to build a wide-bodied plane, the L-1011, and in 1969 contracted with Rolls-Royce to design and manufacture the jet engine, the RB211, for the aircraft. By early 1971 Rolls-Royce, with the job half completed and costs running far ahead of the original projections, nearly went under. To save the contract, Lockheed, itself in financial crisis, had to help Rolls-Royce secure renewed financial backing from the British government. This task meant that Daniel Haughton, Chief Executive of Lockheed Corporation, had to enter into months of negotiations with lateral contracts, all of them external to Lockheed. These included Lord Carrington, the Secretary of State for Defence, Edward Heath, the Prime Minister, Lockheed's bankers and the six US Airlines who had ordered L-1011s and were alarmed at the prospect of either not receiving their planes or being asked to agree to a higher price.

After six months of travelling and meetings, Haughton put together an agreement acceptable to Lockheed and all the lateral parties involved. The British government pledged to pay for all further costs of supplying the engine; Lockheed agreed to pay $180,000 more for each engine; the six customer airlines agreed to pay $140,000 more for each aeroplane; Lockheed's bankers agreed to extend their line of credit, provided the US government guaranteed repayment; and the US Congress approved a bill that guaranteed Lockheed's loans. As Newhouse wrote, Haughton is credited with accomplishing this feat 'by tireless efforts, diplomatic skill, and the fact that he was trusted by all sides'. This example shows how important lateral relationships are to a change agent.

The old cliché, 'it's not what you know but who you know' is both right and wrong when applied to getting Ignition started. What people know, what skills they have, what resources they have, are all vital in the contribution that they can make to the change effort. However it is also important to be keenly aware of what people involved in the change effort don't know or cannot do and it is at this time that who they know becomes crucial. Early warning to the networks of what might be required of them, helps to get them prepared.

COMMIT THE ORGANIZATION

This will probably not be regarded as the most popular strategy for getting started. However, we have seen it being used very effectively. The chief executive of a major financial organization in the UK was trying to jolt his firm into making some long overdue changes. He was not always successful in getting agreement and/or commitment from his management team. The culture of this particular organization was to slow everything down, to be cautious and see how the competitors react to a given issue first. The chief executive adopted an alternative strategy whereby at press conferences or media interviews, he would commit this organization to making certain changes or delivering certain new products or services to their customers by a given date. People within the firm often had little or no idea about this intention, until they read about it in the papers the next day. This strategy led to a lot of frustration, but although people were disgruntled about the way in which Ignition was started, it usually threw the organization into a frenzy of activity, a high energy mode, with key people focusing on what had to be done to deliver the promised product or service to the customers on time. As the promise had been made publicly, by their own chief executive, there was no alternative but to deliver. A service or a product which might traditionally have taken six months to deliver was often delivered in one or two months.

Many organizations view the media with mild paranoia. This particular chief executive used it to get organizational Ignition started by giving clear messages to his customers as to what they could expect and an implied message to his own organization, which was to get started. Often a suspicious attitude results from bad experiences suffered by people who may have been ill-prepared to meet media demands or may be misrepresented by the media. But if used skilfully, the press and television can contribute enormously to Ignition. Bob Geldof used the international media to promote the charity rock concert Live Aid, and the following change in attitude to 'Feed the World'. Conversely, the European pharmaceutical industry has been criticized for always being suspicious and on the defensive with the media rather than taking a more positive approach and, for example, providing the media with examples of its successes. The media can be used very effectively to manage an organization's external image during times of change and development as well as providing the necessary impetus to start somewhere.

Other organizations have used their credos or mission statements to signal the start of a change process. This often sets up expectations in customers and staff alike. The staff may or may not know how they might go about achieving their target, but it gives them a starting point. For example, Caterpillar proclaim a '24 hour parts service anywhere in the world', thus symbolizing an extraordinary commitment to meeting the customers' needs.

There are always good reasons for slowing down the process of change or why the time is not right for getting started. However, as has often been said, change starts with one person, and this one person has to be able to find different ways of enlisting support from others. Committing the organization by telling the press or advertising a certain value e.g. 'the listening bank', forces the change process to get under way. It does not mean that every bank employee will always appear to listen. No doubt there will be some slippage; however it is a standard to aim for and if staff know that their company has been publicly committed to be 'the listening bank' or 'never knowingly undersold' or 'putting people first', then they know that the customers are assessing their behaviour according to a particular slogan. The customers' expectations increase and the staff's awareness of what is required is sharper. We do not necessarily advocate 'committing your organization' without consultation or without support from key people, but some kind of public commitment does focus people's energies towards that particular goal.

CREATE A CRISIS

The chief financial officer of an organization wanted to streamline the budgeting process used by the company. The one currently in use was over complex and never completed on time. A number of attempts were made to try to make the necessary changes, in order to make the process faster and more effective and one that would more accurately reflect the company's reality. Unable to get various parts of the company to use a consistent budgeting process, he announced that the budgeting process for the year had been cancelled and he gave his team a few weeks to come up with usable alternatives. Although this threw the organization into chaos, it also mobilized the required energy to get started on a long overdue process.

It is possible to start Ignition by creating a crisis, but the crisis needs to be well managed and well timed. There is a classic experiment which uses a frog and two containers of water. One container is full of cold water and the other contains boiling water. If the frog is put in the cold water, it does not do anything; however if it is put in hot water, it immediately jumps out. If the container with the frog in cold water is then gently heated, the frog stays in the water. Eventually, as the water gets hotter, the frog dies, because the change in temperature is so gradual that the frog doesn't realize that there is a change. Similarly, too many people in organizations do not sense change or refuse to see it until it is too late. The moral of the story is to get the frogs out of the water by creating a crisis.

Crisis will often provide the required energy and momentum for change. In the early 1980s, Ford Motor Company (USA) was in deep trouble, owing to a number of factors including recession and loss of market share. It was a time of crisis, but Ford changed. Its Ignition is best represented by the success of Ford Taurus in the USA. As a result of the Falklands war, one particular organization was able to use this crisis productively. During a conference, a number of people from British Aerospace reported that individual and team perform-ance shot up by 100 per cent during this war. Although there was no formal recognition or request, engineers and other people involved in repairing aircraft stretched themselves and were prepared to deliver whatever was needed. The key question seemed to be 'What do they require of us to fight this war?' and the key stance seemed to be 'We will make sure we deliver'. Production far exceeded levels that previously had been agreed as optimum and this was without people having to work overtime. A few months later, when one factory was threatened by closure, people looked back at the Falklands war and decided that if they could do it then, it was possible to make those production levels part of their everyday life. A significant change was under way.

Following the same war, fierce controversy broke out over the award of the contract to refit the luxury liner *Cunard Countess* which had been used as a troopship during the war. Shipyards in Britain had been invited to tender for the work which involved refurbishing the ship to return to its peacetime cruise role. They all said it was impossible to meet the 44-day deadline set by Cunard. The Maltese completed the refit within the deadline and in beating all the odds, boosted their yard's morale at a difficult period for all shipyards.

The impetus for change is often dissatisfaction with the way things are at present. The barriers to getting change implemented are often fear of the unknown and fear of the future. While it is true that it is very difficult to get Ignition going in the face of massive resistance, it also seems fatal to wait until all the resistance has been taken care of. In creating a crisis, it is often possible to instigate change because the underlying dissatisfaction may have been articulated. If the dissatisfaction is allowed to continue too long, then the result is more like a revolution than change. Managing a revolution, when feelings of frustration and dissatisfaction are beyond control, is almost impossible. The important thing is to be able to recognize the basic dissatisfactions in the organization and if necessary to heighten them. Dissatisfactions often grow when people in the organization know that there is a threat of competition, or other firms are 'doing better'. Sometimes, getting key people in the organization to visit the competition and see how they do things will create the necessary crisis to get things moving.

CELEBRATE EARLY RESULTS

Especially during times of change, positive feedback is a much stronger motivator than anything else. During times of fast moving change, it is even more important to be able to celebrate early successes, no matter how small they may be. They act as a strong reinforcer to continue the process. Given that change brings with it uncertainty and insecurity, celebrating early successes helps to create an environment in which Ignition can flourish. Managers of change have reported that if they have found it difficult to get change started in one area, for whatever reason, helping to publicize successes in other areas will often result in generating excitement and interest.

Stories that celebrate and publicize success are relished and often serve an important function. They provide vivid pictures, models and examples for other parts of the organization, of the kinds of performance to strive for. The successes and early results made public is also a way of providing reward in the form of recognition. Many companies and in particular their sales teams, now have regular conferences at which high performers are rewarded and recognized. The events are designed to exchange good news, and to associate the forthcoming change with success, fun and excitement.

Rosabeth Moss Kanter in *The Change Masters* talks of making everyone a hero i.e. sharing the recognition that comes from early results. As results begin to show and people begin to behave in ways that will help Ignition, the organization needs to develop other rewards to reinforce these new ways of working. As Blanchard and Johnson have put it, 'Catch them doing something right'.

BADGE MANAGEMENT

Organizations sometimes report that they can't get change started because they don't have a person in a particular role e.g. someone who is going to be responsible for managing the merger between two companies. Giving someone the title 'Merger Coodinator/ Manager' will often get the ball rolling. Calling someone a 'Spark Group Leader' or 'New Product Development Manager' or 'Change Manager', will often get things started. Creating a transition management team can be very important and useful to the change process. It may be wise to appoint a full-time person for the job and give them an appropriate 'badge'. The larger and more complex the change, the more concentrated attention it needs.

REARRANGE THE PHYSICAL ENVIRONMENT

Although it may appear artificial to start changing the physical environment, it certainly can be helpful. Moving desks or filing cabinets, regrouping people, so that individuals who must work together are in closer physical proximity can all help. If Ignition is to take place, then some structures may need to be re-examined and artificial boundaries in the form of screens may need to be broken down as a signal for a different kind of approach or way of working.

With a group of managers from the aerospace industry, who had to restructure in order to ensure survival, the process started by changing the physical environment. They had to restructure to ensure that the aircraft they were making were delivered on time and within budget. We spent three days with this team of managers, planning the transition and clarifying the new roles and responsibilities. Yet they found it difficult to get started on their task. In the end, the clearest signal they could give to other people in the plant about the reorganization, to ensure that it was recognized that there was going to be a different way of working, was by changing the physical environment. Sure enough, from then on, they were able to implement other change plans. Changing the physical environment in itself doesn't make the change happen, but it does get it started.

Sir John Harvey-Jones in his recent book *Making it Happen* reports that when he became chairman of ICI, he wished to make some changes in the board and the way it was made up. One starting point was to try to get rid of the Millbank headquarters. Although in the end this was not feasible, it was a signal to the rest of the organization of other changes to come. Sir John Harvey-Jones cited another example of symbolic change: his alteration not only of the pattern of board meetings, but also the venue. 'The day that I assumed responsibility as chairman, instead of meeting, as we always had done, in the ICI boardroom, an imposing but somewhat impractical room, we met in what had been my office. The boardroom had been designed in an earlier era to emphasize the power of the Chairman and this was not at all the way that I wanted to run the company. I wanted our executive team to operate as a band of brothers where discussion was free and uninhibited, where people could get up and walk around, pour themselves a cup of coffee, argue, draw things on flip charts, gesticulate, and generally feel easy and unrestricted. None of these things had been possible in our magnificent boardroom. Indeed, it was almost impossible to get an argument generated across the imposing round table which, while ensuring from one point of view that everybody could see everybody else, also ensured that the distances were so large that it was difficult to see each other close to. Other changes that I made were that when we met, we sat in comfortable conference chairs, each of which had small adjustable side table on which one could place a collection of papers. There was no organization to where we sat, each person taking the nearest convenient chair. We had flip charts, tea and coffee etc. all available and we met, more often than not, in shirt sleeves. These things may seem unimportant, but in generating the atmosphere for change such details have a critical cumulative effect.'

LOOK AT THE SITUATION THROUGH NEW EYES

Unless a company is progressing all the time, it will in effect start moving backwards because other companies will take over. We only have to think of the British motorcycle industry and its once key position, to see the false belief that it could sustain a position of world leadership without innovation. Changing things around the edges is often not enough. While such world-famous companies as BSA and Triumph were modestly adjusting their models, which had been at the leading edge, the Japanese, and particularly Honda, looked at the situation through new eyes. They didn't accept the limitations and constraints that the British world position had led us to assume. They reasoned, correctly, that a substantial increase in the revolutions per minute of the engine would increase the power to weight ratio and permit a whole range of new developments. They were able to do this, and the results for the British motorcycle industry are well documented. Interestingly, when Honda's position was threatened by other Japanese companies and they began to lose market share, their instant reaction was to increase the rate of innovation. In one year they launched more new models than all their leading competitors put together.

Staying in the same position is without doubt the most comfortable position in the short term, but it is also the highest risk strategy for the company. There are many examples of companies which have failed to look at the situation through fresh eyes. They may have believed that they had found 'the answer' and stayed with that particular solution too long, while the competition was stimulated to greater Ignition and overtaking the particular company. An outstanding example of this is the Swiss watch industry. It was the Swiss who developed perfection in mechanical and automatic watches. They believed they could view the emerging competition from Japan as an attack in their traditional field and so felt secure in the knowledge that they could defend themselves. They ignored, almost fatally, the development of the electronic watch and were nearly forced out of the battle altogether as a result. However, they fought back successfully with the SWATCH innovation.

ANTICIPATE

Basically, organizations need to get Ignition going so that they can stay ahead of their competitors, so that they can maintain a leading edge over other firms. Looking ahead at what might be around the corner is a good place to get started. Anticipation often helps to reduce anxiety and mobilize action. Thinking through what the worst scenario might be can do two things. Firstly, it somehow removes fear from the situation and secondly it gets people into action mode. During times of Ignition there are a lot of surprises. Anticipation can take place in many ways. It is not just a reflective activity. Today organizations are finding out what might be around the corner by learning from getting out and about their own company, talking to and observing the competition, looking at the best practice, reading, gathering what other people know about it and keeping a close eye on forecasts and trends. We were present at a management seminar held for a group of British Airways managers when the news about the British Airways/British Caledonian merger was announced. Amidst the excitement and the apprehension, one of the first things that these managers did was to pool what they knew about British Caledonian – both the positive and the negative aspects, names and telephone numbers of contacts they had in the other airline and any other data they could remember about it. From nowhere, within 30 minutes we had masses of information and data. The managers could start using this immediately in preparation for their role in managing the merger successfully.

Resistance to change often leads people in organizations not to anticipate accurately and this inevitably leads to losing the leading edge. The London docks are a good example: it was resistance to change which led employers to persist with casual labouring practices so long after they had become extinct everywhere else. The dock workers themselves resisted any new introduction of work methods. In marked contrast is the reaction of Rotterdam to changes in technology such as mechanical handling of containerization. The results are easy to see. London Docklands took a long time to become a development site for housing and new business while Rotterdam has been Europe's largest port for some time.

The ability to think ahead and anticipate events will often help to get into action mode. It is a capacity to pick up signals constantly, to see what is going on out there and link this to what might also be known intuitively. This in turn often forms the outline of what the implications might be and what may need to be done about it. Researchers at Shell found that the only consistent factor that distinguished the more effective managers from their less effective colleagues was the ability to take the 'helicopter view'. This is the ability to rise above day-to-day events and pressures and take a broader view of what is going on and what is likely to happen. It is like taking an aerial snapshot of the situation and being able to see connections between supposedly unrelated events. This often helps to anticipate the next move.

People in organizations must be aware of the need for change and also realize the high risk in not changing. The glittering prizes go to the forerunners; in organizations where Ignition is part of everyday life, people are continually on the look-out for signs which may tell them that they might be losing the lead position. People in this type of company recognize the signs and start drawing them to the attention of their senior management, long before the competition realize that they are catching up. But if a company enjoys a long period out in front, these anticipating senses often get dulled. People then become unaware of the dangers surrounding them. We only have to think of the Singer Sewing Machine Company, a name which became synonymous with the product it made. Similarly, the generic term of the vacuum cleaner is still a Hoover. Yet both these companies have lost their lead position and now face intense competition.

Anticipation requires people in organizations to balance the use of their intuition with their rational skills. For example someone may have a hunch as to what new product a particular market needs, but he or she needs to test this out with all the data that the market researchers are putting out. Anticipation used together with the available data is a very powerful combination to get things started.

REASONS FOR NOT STARTING

In working with many different companies over the years, we have been given many reasons for not getting started. Sometimes they are valid, sometimes they are a technique for buying more time and at other times it is simply resistance to change. The list below is by no means comprehensive, but may ring warning bells if Ignition is being blocked in a particular organization.

1. We tried that once before.
2. Our situation is different.
3. Think how much it will cost.
4. That's beyond our responsibility.
5. We're too busy at the moment.
6. That's not my job
7. It's too radical a change
8. We don't have time
9. We would need too much help
10. It makes equipment obsolete
11. Let's test it thoroughly
12. Our plant is too small
13. Not practical for operations
14. The men will never accept it
15. We've never done that before
16. Wait until the unions hear that
17. It's outside company policy
18. Runs up our overheads
19. We don't have the authority
20. That's too 'ivory tower'
21. That's not the main problem
22. Let's get back to reality
23. It works – why change it?
24. Is this your own idea?
25. You're quite right – but . . .
26. You're ahead of your time
27. We're not ready for that
28. We don't have room
29. It isn't in the budget
30. Can't teach an old dog new tricks
31. Good idea, but impractical
32. Let's keep this up our sleeves
33. Head Office wouldn't go for it
34. Send me a memo about this

35. I would like to sleep on it
36. We would be the laughing stock
37. Not that one again
38. We have to look at the longer term
39. Where did you dig that one up?
40. O.K. – leave it with me
41. That's what you can expect from staff
42. There is a time and a place for everything
43. Why don't we discuss it over some lunch?
44. Let's form a working party
45. Has anyone else tried it?
46. I don't see the connection
47. What you're really saying is . . .
48. I thought you would have more sense
49. What do they do in other plants?
50. I know that it can't be done
51. If anyone could do it, you could, but . . .
52. Just think of the paperwork involved
53. Its been on order for ages
54. You know as well as I do that . . .
55. Tell him to ring back later
56. That's confidential at the moment
57. Engineering are reviewing it
58. But this is not the USA
59. That's not the way we do things here
60. Who could we get to do that?
61. When you've been here as long as me . . .
62. I wouldn't have thought it was possible
63. There was a time when we used to . . .
64. You know I would help if I could
65. Let me give you a small piece of advice
66. I take it you want me to be frank
67. You don't realize how complicated our industry really is
68. The chief executive is on vacation
69. It has been done before
70. It won't work
71. Let's just finish this project first

72. It would need too many people
73. We can't afford it
74. We are not ready for it yet
75. It's all right in theory but can you put it into into practice?
76. Too academic
77. Too modern
78. Too old-fashioned
79. It needs careful consideration
80. Let's wait until the new boss joins
81. Let's form a committee
82. Let's think it over for a while and watch developments
83. The union will scream
84. Let's put it in writing
85. Won't work in our department
86. Our department is too small for that
87. Our department is too big for that
88. We can't do it under the regulations
89. It's too early
90. It's too late
91. It will offend
92. People won't accept it.
93. The boss won't like it
94. The customers won't like it
95. Our suppliers couldn't cope with it
96. This isn't the right time
97. How will we sell it to production?
98. We'll have to check with Head Office
99. It would mean admitting we've got it wrong before
100. But we've put so much effort into getting the existing process working well

START SOMEWHERE

Listed below are some ways in which the Ignition process can be started:

- Talk about it.

- Don't worry about it being perfect first time round.

- Give it a name or a symbol.

- Have you talked to them?

- Mobilize the network.

- Commit the organization.

- Create a crisis.

- Celebrate early results.

- Use badge management. Give someone an appropriate title.

- Re-arrange the physical environment.

- Look the change in the eye. Don't be caught looking the wrong way.

- Anticipate.

- Look out for reasons for not starting. They can be a stalling mechanism.

References

- *International Management*, December 1982.

- Peters, T.J. and Waterman, R.H. (1982) *In Search of Excellence*, New York: Harper and Row.

- Waterman, R.H. (1987) *The Renewal Factor*, London: Bantam.

- Naisbitt, J. and Aburdene, P. (1985) *Reinventing the Corporation*, New York: Warner Books.

- Moss Kanter, R. (1985) *The Change Masters*, London: Unwin Hyman.

- Newhouse, J., The New Yorker. *'The Sporting Game'* July 1982

- Car and Driver 1986

- Motor Trend 1986

- Hastings, C., Bixby, P., Chaudhry-Lawton, R. (1986) *Super-teams*, London: Fontana.

- Harvey-Jones, J. (1988) *Making it Happen – Reflections on Leadership*, London: Collins.

- Goldberg, P. (1983) *The Intuitive Edge*, Los Angeles: Jeremy P. Tarcher Inc. New York: St Martin's Press.

- Blanchard, K., Spencer, J. (1982) *The One Minute Manager*, New York: William Morrow and Company, inc.

6. Spark Groups

'Teamworking is mainstream management of the business.'
Sir John Egan, Chief Executive, BAA plc

Why is teamworking becoming so important? What is the reason behind the success of small teams, demonstrated over and over again in industry and commerce? The answer is simple. People like working in small teams. The small team model is the most popular alternative to hierarchical and bureaucratic organizations. They come in many different guises. The key ingredients seem to be flexible, fast, small and talented. Small groups can accomplish even more when people with different backgrounds, talents and disciplines are brought together to work on a problem, a new product or an organizational change.

Fortune magazine's eight most innovative companies in America – American Airlines, Apple, Campbell Soup, GE, Intel, Merck, 3M and Phillip Morris – are all experts at using multi-disciplinary and cross-functional teams for innovation, problem-solving and change. People in different disciplines are simply not allowed to remain in isolation, writes *Fortune*. 'Business units are kept small in part to throw engineers, marketers and financial experts together into the sort of tight groups often found in start-up companies'.

Large Corporations – Small Groups
Apple Computers is an American success story in the rags-to-riches tradition. Steven Jobs and Stephen Woznaik were more interested in

154

making devices that could tap into the telephone system for free calls. They never made any such equipment, but somewhere in the tinkering they came up with an idea and a system for a simple computer and they chose a simple name for it: Apple. Apple caught the big giants, IBM, Xerox and Digital unaware and grabbed the lion's share of the PC market. Apple Computer Co was formed in 1977 and went public in 1980. The story of how the firm started is well documented. Apple did things differently; the partners started in a garage, then set up in a separate building with a small team of talented people and produced PC after PC that was a best seller. It publicized itself as a different kind of company which was values-driven. The small team's way of working was the Apple way of working.

Many large companies have seen small businesses get ahead in the market place. IBM, one of the best managed companies in the world, watched Digital Equipment take the lead in minicomputers and Apple in personal computers. Clearly the tried, trusted and previously successful IBM strategies were not working in the current environment. The market place seemed to favour small businesses who could move fast without bureaucratic constraints.

As a result, a lot of companies like IBM, Xerox and NCR are formulating new ways of working. Their aim is to use and apply what is best about small businesses – teamworking, speed of response, flexibility, innovation – and add these to their own strength of stability and financial security.

IBM's response to Apple was to duplicate as closely as possible the environment that generated the creativity behind Apple's success. IBM created a number of 'Independent Business Units'. These were teams outside the company's normal structure, designed to be small and flexible enough to be able to respond to the extremely volatile high-tech marketplace. 'If you are competing against people who started in a garage, you have to start in a garage', says Don Estridge, who led the IBU that came up with the PC. Estridge took a group of 12 people, on a limited budget, working in highly unattractive surroundings in Florida, people who had a lot of energy and zeal and also enjoyed freedom from the IBM headquarters in New York. This group created the IBM PC in a much shorter time-frame than anything else IBM had produced in years. IBM people think that this approach combines the best of both worlds, giving stability with speed.

In the book *The Soul of a New Machine* author Tracy Kidder vividly describes the kind of high-energy small team innovation at Data General in Westborough, Massachusetts. Kidder's account describes a small team's huge struggle to dominate a machine. The working of the 32 bit mini-computer Eagle was a massive task. It demanded every waking hour of a brilliant and aggressive team of young computer wizards who worked for the multi-million dollar company Data General. They were given one year: each day the 'microkids' tested their physical, psychological and technical abilities to the limit. They finally commanded the machine's obedience and delivered the Eagle. There is much to be learned from how this team operated.

Lessons of organizational Ignition can be seen in industries other than high-tech. Ford Motor Company, after years of producing products that did not sell well, finally embarked on a programme in the early 80s to build the highly successful Taurus. Ford decided to do things differently with Taurus. Management showed the tentative designs to the workforce and asked for their help in devising a car that would be easy to build. The Taurus Team was formed under the direction of Lou Veraldi. All the different necessary disciplines were brought together to interact and contribute from the start. The Taurus team brought in a winning product. The car won *Motor Trade Magazine's* 1986 Car of the Year award. It generated Ignition in the whole company.

Two examples illustrate clearly how small groups can be used to accelerate change. In one case, Ford employees formed a group to tackle a problem that they had experienced for two years. No matter what they did to adjust the carpet properly on the car floor, there was always a bulge. The engineering department had had the problem referred to them but had not been able to come up with a solution. Within three months the new group found a way of cutting a small slit in the carpet in just the right place, and the bulge disappeared. In three months they had solved a problem that the engineering department had not been able to solve in two years.

Fast implementation is absolutely necessary in order to maintain the competitive edge. It is not something that Ford was used to. The Taurus team found a different way of handling this, leading Dick Ross, Ford's Chicago plant personnel officer to say 'Two months ago it was like Beirut in here. Everything was levelled'. They quite literally tore down all the walls. In the biggest single change ever made by Ford, they shut the plant down, gutted it, replaced everything with new technology and had it back in operation producing the new Taurus, in just under three months.

SLIMS, the Sunlife Investment Management Group, was launched similarly. A small group of highly talented people, headed by an outsider, Alan Frost, was given the go-ahead by the more conservative parent to launch the new company. It was seen as a satellite with a lifeline from the mother ship available if required. Within a few months, they were one of the most successful fund management groups in Britain. They did things differently from the parent company. Focused, flexible, following-through, fast and action-orientated would be appropriate words to describe this highly successful team.

W.L. Gore and Associates Inc. manufactures Gore-tex fabric which is now much used as a sports and military material. Gore-tex keeps out rain but allows the body to breathe. Founder Bill Gore set out in 1958 to create a profitable company which would reproduce the sense of excitement and commitment that he had felt as a member of a small task force when he was working in the research labs of E.I. Du Pont de Nemours. The Gore example shows how companies are trying to transform energy into a creative and enterprising spirit and channel it into small workgroups where communication is quicker and more effective.

In Japan, an 'inside-the-company-venture' was established at Hitachi in 1983. Earlier that year, Hitachi's president, Katsushige Mita, was approached by the managing director, Ozeki, and asked to create a special plant for office automation equipment, 'in order to make up for the company's serious delay in the field'. Instead of looking at whether or not such a plant would be profitable, Mita said 'why don't you build a small shed and start from there as our predecessors did, when they founded the company?' This sounds very similar to what IBM's Don Estridge said when he had to find a way of competing with Apple's PC.

The *Japan Economic Journal* points out that it takes 30-40 minutes for a tanker weighing 300,000 tons to change its course. In the same way big companies find it difficult to adapt swiftly to changes. In the present age of high-tech, when whirlwind innovations and the resultant drastic changes in industrial structures are the order of the day, a common and rigid structure can easily cost a company its life. Task groups and inside-the-company ventures are being used in companies throughout Japan. 'We are trying to turn existing organizations into new venture units' says another company president.

Sharp Corporation has used small groups to spearhead the company's new product development. Sharp has a special group of about 300 researchers, as well as 5,000 engineers. The researchers are divided into sub-groups of ten people and each can freely select its members. No manager in the company can refuse requests from the leader of the sub-group. Each sub-group spearheads a new product development by taking full advantage of the company's human and other resources.

Innovative companies are exploring different ways and a range of different structures including multi-disciplinary teams to promote better communication, innovation and increased productivity, and to embrace change rapidly. However, there is no one answer which will fit every situation and every company culture. No matter how well thought out a particular way of working or a structure may be, ultimately the company must experiment with new structures and tailor-make the structure to its own specific needs.

The people who know most about any job are the ones who are actually doing it. The challenge for business today is to be able to harness that energy, to tap into the information and apply it widely. Companies are recognizing that the way career paths have been traditionally set up means that good technical people and specialists often have to leave the area of work they know best and excel at, in order to get to a higher level job which offers more power, influence and rewards. Not everyone makes a good manager, but many would have been better off and much happier if they had continued doing the work they love to do best. The forced moved into the management structure can result in a great loss of vital creative energy for the company. Companies are recognizing this, e.g. IBM has developed a fellowship option that lets engineers remain engineers while at the same time being able to make progress in status, pay and other company perks. Their job is not to worry about management progression, but to be creative and innovative and put their energy and commitment behind what really interests them.

According to Peters and Waterman, small groups are 'quite simply, the building blocks of excellent companies'. The section on 'large companies – small groups' shows how small groups have been used very successfully by a number of companies to innovate and problem solve. In working with different organizations over the past few years, we have reached the conclusion that the small group process can be used very effectively to accelerate Ignition. However these groups must be capable of responding quickly to the problem or the change. Peters and Waterman report that 'one multi-billion dollar corporation found to its amazement that it had 325 task forces in existence and that not a single task force had completed its charge in the last 3 years.' In this chapter we highlight some of the key areas that need attention if groups are to be used effectively to accelerate Ignition. We have labelled these groups 'Spark Groups'.

Spark Groups

Spark Groups can be used at all different stages of Ignition. For example, a Spark Group might initially be used to visualize the change that needs to take place, to gather data from other organizations in the industry, to examine the key ingredients of the required change and how they would fit into the current organization. At a later stage, they might be used to translate the vision into an implementation plan within different areas of the organization, ensuring involvement and commitment from a larger number of people. Finally, Spark Groups can be used to monitor the change and scan the environment for other data which might lead to further change and innovation.

In a previous book, *The Superteam Solution*, we have described some of the guidelines for outstanding teams. These would have a lot of relevance to the Spark Group. Described below are key lessons that we have drawn from observing other groups at work, working with our clients and forming our ideas about how Spark Groups can be most effectively used for Ignition and accelerating the change process in organizations.

What are Spark Groups?

A Spark Group is our term for a group of people behaving in a particular way, approaching problems in a way that helps to boost organizational Ignition. The group needs to be small if the Spark-like qualities are to be obtained. They must focus sharply on a given problem. Either the problem could be assigned to the Spark Group or it could be initiated by a group or an individual.

Spark Groups do not last long. They have limited life. Their role is to mix the Air and Fuel to generate energy and move organizational Ignition forward but they are not there to try to stretch out their existence.

Spark Groups can exist at all and any levels in the organization. If Ignition is to take place then there may need to be several Spark Groups throughout the company. However, they can be generated either from within a department or by bringing together people from different departments or different disciplines. Departmental Spark Groups and multi-functional Spark Groups adopt similar behaviour, although the problems they work on will vary.

As Spark Groups only have a limited life, they also have the ability of forming, breaking up and then reforming when the need arises. Depending on the nature of the problem or issue that this Spark Group is attempting to address, it may need some of the same people but also others who bring different knowledge, skills or attributes may be more useful. Forming and reforming Spark Groups helps to include more people rather than making it an exclusive or elitist activity, and to generate a different kind of mentality in the organization, contributing towards teamwork, individual development and breaking down functional or specialist boundaries that have become barriers.

Spark Groups can also clarify what they are trying to achieve and how they will know they have been successful. They set both tangible and intangible measures for themselves. The first key measure is usually time. They address such questions as how long do we need to exist as a Spark Group to get this job done, or this problem solved?

In summary, Spark Groups are small groups of people, who come together for a limited amount of time, to focus on a particular problem. They can come from within a particular discipline or be a multi-disciplinary group. Their key aim is to generate energy and momentum for organizational Ignition.

How can Spark Groups help organizations?

As Spark Groups work on specific areas, issues or problems, the speed with which a large number of issues can be tackled increases. A side-effect of generating this type of group to help organizational change is of course getting a large number of people involved, committed and contributing to the change effort simultaneously. It also means that different Spark Groups can approach specific change from a number of directions and explore the many different angles, thus ensuring that the change has stability and a much greater and faster chance of successful implementation.

It is often reasonably easy to deal with the symptoms of a problem, but not quite so easy to determine the cause. A Spark Group with responsibilities for focusing on one specific problem is more likely to be able to determine the cause. If the group is generated carefully (i.e. by choosing the right people) and the problem or issue assigned has been well thought out, the chances are that setting up the Spark Group will concentrate the efforts of those people who would be trying to solve the problem anyway.

Spark Groups, if used appropriately in organizations, can help to resolve significant issues and reach decisions. If an issue is important or considered a priority, then giving a Spark Group responsibility to resolve it will often achieve positive results, rather than diluting the effect by making it the responsibility of a whole department or division. If the Spark Group is sufficiently skilled and staffed with competent people, then the chances are greater that they will also be able to resolve decisions that cross functional or organizational boundaries. Of course the key skill here is the ability to influence peers, subordinates and superiors in areas where Spark Group members have no direct authority.

Unusual situations often require unusual and different ways of operating. Spark Groups can be used to deal with unusual situations. They have to live outside the normal organization structure, and this provides an added source of energy. They are not meant as a threat or an alternative to the established structure. They can exist in parallel, one feeding off the other.

As the Spark Group gets more competent and confident, it can overlap conventional organization boundaries instead of being seen as something totally different. The skill that the Spark Group members need to learn is the ability to see themselves, and behave in such a way that others see them, as being able to be members of different groups, teams or functions at the same time, without one role threatening another.

Expectations

Using Spark Groups as one way of accelerating change or resolving problems gives rise to some expectations that need to be met, both by the Group and the organization. Firstly, it is important that Spark Groups are assembled to resolve non-routine, important issues. If they are set up to deal with routine issues, it is likely that this will cut against functional and organizational boundaries, thus building up resistance. The exceptional and important aspects of the issues will help to concentrate efforts and focus people's minds on the problem at hand. If the problem is also critical and urgent, that really can help to generate energy. It brings into focus all the types of behaviour necessary to deliver results. The expectation very clearly needs to be that it is the urgent, important, critical and non-routine issues that Spark Groups are dealing with.

A key criterion to measure the Spark Group's success is that it must deliver a concrete, well thought out implementation plan, not just recommendations. Recommendations are subject to change and more likely to be left on the shelf, unactioned. If an organization is using Spark Groups as a way of dealing with certain types of problem, it also needs to ensure that it is prepared to implement the findings. The Spark Group's work in turn does not end with putting forward an implementation plan. They must expect to follow through and ensure successful implementation. In turn, this brings us back to how they are staffed. Spark Groups must be staffed by competent people if implementation is to be achieved. If this condition is not met, the chances of a Group fulfilling its mandate are slim. Elsewhere we have mentioned that senior and middle managers cannot exclude themselves from Spark Groups (see page 167). Spark Groups need senior managers to sponsor them. The sponsor must be prepared and committed to carry out the implementation plan. If this is not clearly understood and accepted as part and parcel of generating the Groups, they will soon lose their credibility as well as the energy and commitment that follows successful implementation.

When to start a Spark Group

Start a Spark Group as soon as a need is recognized. Waiting for more information, the correct structure, the appropriate process, terms of reference or any other reason that may delay the start of a Spark Group will often set the foundations for further delay and reaction. When a need is recognized, that is the time when the energy is most focused and concentrated on understanding and dealing with the issue. Once the Spark Group is created, it is probably best to let its members decide what they need in terms of information, structure, process etc. Often not much preparation is needed. Most of the questions (or the relevant information) are often in the head of the senior manager or the person acting as the sponsor. Members need to be able to help the sponsor articulate this information and use those bits of the data that are useful for their purposes. However, when starting a Spark Group, it is often important to specify the starting and the end date. This helps the members to structure their planning as well as providing a deadline and ensuring the 'limited life' quality of the group. If the Spark Group can be given any other success criteria at this stage, that can be helpful; however it is not essential, as the members, if working effectively, will generate their own criteria for success as well as asking the sponsor for his/her views. The key thing at this stage is to get started and not to lose momentum that is often there when a problem or a need is recognized.

Who should be part of the Spark Group?

There are a number of different criteria that need to be kept in mind when generating a Spark Group, whose importance varies according to the kind of problem or issue that is the subject matter. Who, then, should be part of the Group?

- People who are most knowledgeable about the subject.

- People who may have insight or different views on the subject.

- People who are close to the subject; who are dealing with it every day and intimately

- Those who would be affected by the issue under discussion

- Someone who has some clout or source of power, which will be particularly helpful when it comes to implementation

- Individuals who want to be part of the Spark Group, either because they can own the required change, or they have the energy to contribute towards its resolution, or they are committed and enthusiastic about the subject and about being part of the group. Other individuals may seek membership for personal reasons. These can vary from seeing it as a development opportunity, a way of getting visibility, or wanting to be part of a Spark Group because it is important to be seen to be part of one. Whatever the motivation, if the individual is willing, energetic and enthusiastic, it can help progress.

- Individuals who bring specific skills or abilities that may be useful

- Individuals who are persuasive in their style or able to influence people in other ways acceptable in that particular organization.

People who are creative and have the ability to generate different options and also those people who have a 'can do' attitude.

Sometimes members will choose themselves, and at other times, a sponsor or a Spark Group leader may be responsible for selecting the members. It is important to ensure that some of the above-mentioned criteria are met in order to give the group the best chance of success.

How Many?

Between six and eight members appear to be an ideal number. If there are fewer, they would probably have to work extremely hard to deliver on the change project, and might feel very fragmented. It is also difficult to ensure a good mix of the relevant skills and abilities required for the particular project. If the numbers in the Group are much higher, it is more difficult to ensure that everyone is contributing effectively. The quieter or shyer members may find it harder to contribute in a large group, and thus the Group may not be able to tap into their experience and expertise. It is also difficult to harness the energy of much larger groups quickly, because the simple process of listening to each person's point of view and ensuring a fair hearing takes up a lot of time. Small group research has consistently concluded that seven, plus or minus two, is the most appropriate group size. Secondly, addressing the question of who needs to be there will also help to determine the Spark Group size. It is important to answer the question who needs to be there honestly, rather than giving in to 'if we don't include him/her, she/he will be upset'. Members must want to be part of the Spark Group, and carrying passengers who really have little to contribute or little energy for the activity will only slow things down.

A way of selecting may be to ensure that the members you have chosen are active and concerned participants only. 'Definitely no observers' must also be a rule. Having an observer as part of the group adds different pressures and dynamics. As described here, the best way of getting to know how a group operates (if that is the motivation of the observer) is to be an active participant. If an individual has the motivation and energy, then he or she will usually have something to contribute. Adding observers will increase numbers, making it more difficult in many different ways, not least in getting the group to meet at a certain time, given that the people involved are likely to have busy jobs too. It is best to start a Spark Group with the ideal number i.e. six to eight. It is quite possible to add someone to the group when specialists' input is needed. Temporary membership by specialists is likely to be more useful and effective than starting with a large group.

Spark Group Leader

This is an important role, if the success of a Spark Group is to be ensured. The person can be appointed by the sponsor or selected by the other group members. What means of selection are used will of course vary, depending on the kind of problem – Ignition, the organization culture etc. However it is important to highlight some of the criteria that are useful when considering who should be a Spark Group leader. The leader does not necessarily have to possess detailed knowledge or have expertise in the subject under discussion. The skill and expertise in leading groups of people is a much higher priority than technical expertise.

The Spark Group leader needs to be an individual who can move people towards action. The orientation towards short diagnostic cycles and rapid implementation is necessary for accelerated change (see page 159). The leader has an important role in judging the fine line between not killing creativity and option generation, and ensuring that the group does move towards action and implementation at a reasonable speed.

Sometimes Spark Groups can produce ideas which may be attractive but not necessarily workable within the culture and context in which they exist. If the leader is able to draw on broad business and management experience, then the chances of being able to determine the workability of a particular idea is higher. The leader needs to be closely in tune with the rest of the organization, understanding the underlying values and the culture without being blinkered by current practices. Having 'organization savvy' will not only help to keep the group on track but also ensure that there is some 'reality checking' as the group proceeds with its task.

The leader must be a skilled conductor, i.e. possessing the ability to coordinate and synchronize individual capabilities, talents and ideas. This entails listening carefully, pulling together ideas, looking for patterns where patterns haven't existed previously and above all letting every member of the Spark Group influence the discussion. If the Spark Group leader has a tendency to influence or drive the discussion in a particular direction, she/he may not be using the detailed knowledge and expertise that individual members bring to the party.

Managing the boundaries between functions or departments or indeed with any other interested groups both inside and outside the parent organization will take up a lot of the leader's time. She/he needs to be comfortable with conflict and finding ways of resolving differences rather than ignoring them or running away from them. It is possible that the leader may be the sole member in contact with the sponsor. In this case she/he needs to be able to articulate the success criteria as determined by the Spark Group, clarify expectations that the sponsor may have and also negotiate for more tangible resources such as time, money and equipment. Effective influencing skills and interpersonal skills are essential tools for the leader.

Sponsoring a Spark Group

Sponsoring a Spark Group does not mean that that person has to be a member of that group. This role requires the person to be a godfather, a mentor, a troubleshooter, a fixer and a smoother. Sponsoring a Spark Group is not a passive activity. Apart from direct contact with the group leader and the members, the sponsor is also a key link person between the Spark Group and the rest of the organization.

A sponsor may be the person who generates a Spark Group. The reason for this initiative can vary from a problem which needs resolving, to finding new ways of dealing with a situation, to implementing a part of the more long-term change that may be under way in different parts of the organization.

Because of the nature of the role, a sponsor is invariably a senior manager who is able to generate a Spark Group and provide the necessary tangible and intangible support that may be needed. The sponsor's commitment to the group is a vital factor in determining its success. The sponsor is often required to be persuasive, to use political savvy and to have the endurance and determination to ensure that the implementation plan as put forward by the group is actioned. Being committed to such a project does have a price tag attached to it. It does imply that tangible resources like time, money and more intangible ones like support, persuasion and so on will be required, and it falls on the sponsor to be able to find these resources.

Spark Groups often generate new information which may have strategic implications. While the group's role may be at the tactical level, the sponsor needs to be able to feed the strategic implications into the appropriate arena.

Several components form the commitment required by the sponsor. The sponsor needs to believe in the project or change effort that the group is undertaking while at the same time having an in-depth understanding of the impact of this change and its implications for the rest of the organization. The sponsor also needs to be able to identify the group or groups of people within the organization who may be affected by these changes. Often a Spark Group's effort will come to a standstill if the sponsor has not appreciated that resources like time, money, commitment and people will be needed for a successful change effort: the sponsor must be able to commit these resources to the project. Obviously the sponsor has to demonstrate strong support and commitment to the group and the tasks it is undertaking, while privately being willing and able to meet the leader and/or members in order to clarify, negotiate and convey support. Regardless of what the group is doing, the sponsor jeopardizes the change if his/her commitment falters.

During different phases of the group's life, the sponsor has to utilize different skills. In the early stages, effective communication between leader and sponsor is particularly important. It requires both to define clearly and agree the criteria for success. It also requires these two people to be able to negotiate and agree standards and acceptable levels of operating. Both parties must also be able to listen effectively and start the process of building trust at this early stage.

At the next stage, the sponsor needs an appreciation and understanding of the diversity that may exist between what the group is doing and the rest of the organization. The sponsor will have to utilize all his/her interpersonal skills in order to create a climate in which differences can be discussed, and to bring his/her organizational experiences to bear by helping the group to understand the culture within which the ideas must thrive. Effective communication and being able to listen to diverse views alone is not enough to get the implemenatation process started. The sponsor must be the key link person helping to integrate these different views. The skill required by the sponsor here is the ability to live with ambiguity, as the Spark Group may not be able to provide answers or reasons for everything. The sponsor will have to pursue new possibilities with an open mind and modify his/her own view, beliefs and behaviour in order to support the change, and at the same time be able to discriminate and identify issues and concepts which cannot be integrated.

In the final phases of the Spark Group's life, (although some of these activities need to start early), the sponsor will have to harness the momentum and energy generated by the group and channel it towards successful implementation. The skills of the sponsor and his/her time and commitment are of utmost importance here. Specific goals regarding the implementation process must be established, progress monitored and any reinforcement necessary to ensure successful implementation provided. The sponsor must be acutely aware of how the implementation plan will affect various people in the organization, and may need to proceed with the implementation at a speed and in a manner that takes care of the needs and concerns of people. Above all, the sponsor must be able to modify the implementation plan, in discussion with the Group throughout its life to assure its relevance to the current organizational reality, without using that as an excuse or as a way of blocking implementation.

Finally the sponsor must have the skill to manage the consequences of the change effort. This will include managing the organizational, political and personal consequences that may arise as a result of the implementation of the Group's plans.

Reward, recognition and reinforcement are extremely important if Spark Groups are to continue generating energy. The sponsor is usually the first 'external' source on which the group tests its ideas. Recognition and support from the sponsor are extremely important but sometimes neglected or ignored. Not only does the sponsor provide a source of feedback, but may at times be the only source of reward and recognition. The sponsor should be alert to this and be prompt in giving reward and recognition when appropriate and also constructive feedback when the Spark Group's activities may not be appropriate, may not meet the agreed goals, may be letting deadlines slip or engaging in behaviour which is not acceptable.

The sponsor's role is not an easy one and it certainly is not passive. Sponsoring a Spark Group can be time-consuming but extremely rewarding, challenging and exciting.

Spark Groups without the Sparkle

Two examples are worth describing to demonstrate how in two situations, the Spark Groups did not quite work. In one instance 'support groups' were created during a week-long corporate management programme. Managers from all levels, functions and disciplines attended the programme, which formed part of a larger culture change effort. During the week, people worked on various projects in groups of seven or eight. Each group had a consultant/tutor attached to it. After the programme, the support groups were encouraged to meet, creating their own time and finding their own resources. They were to meet to support each other in carrying forward the messages of the corporate programme.

One of the first problems was the fact that the support group members were often at different corners of the globe. Some of the more enterprising members found a way round that by combining a business trip with a support group meeting. Others were less successful. The success of the support group idea was mixed. After the initial high of the programme and promises of 'we must meet within the next month', when the group did meet they still had things to talk about from the programme and feedback from questionnaires received after the programme was to be shared. Thereafter, the support groups fizzled out rapidly. They did not seem to be serving a purpose any more. Having to keep them alive was a lot harder work. Perhaps if some of the principles of Spark Groups, i.e. limited life, dealing with a specific issue, being action-orientated etc. could have been applied, these support groups could have contributed more fully to the Ignition for culture change in this company. Unstructured, with no objective or purpose, the support groups were of limited value. What they did was to go some way towards breaking down organization barriers and give a little more insight to people about what other functions did. In our opinion, this was a missed opportunity; the groups were fired up and ready to contribute, but they needed a focus.

The second example is somewhat different. Here the task forces were set up in a small but highly successful architectural design company. The groups had a specific focus and were asked to do certain things within given time frames. It seemed as if setting up the groups had released energy within that organization and they achieved more in a few weeks than the organization had achieved in a number of years put together. Their problems arose when they tried to start the implementation. The sponsors of these groups were senior managers, who were also the founding fathers of the company. While they were keen to get Ignition going in the company and happy to set up Spark Groups, they weren't ready to manage the consequences and what it meant for them. Fear and insecurity gripped them as the young executives were seen to be taking over and pushing the organization in a direction perhaps not thought of by the founding fathers. The blocks appeared in strange ways e.g. not being able to get an appointment with the sponsor for a presentation on the outcome of the project, or the paper was not written in the style that the sponsors were used to and so on. In this case the Spark Groups were working extremely efficiently but faltering commitment from the sponsors, driven by fear, insecurity and perhaps not enough involvement by the Spark Group leader, led to problems at the time when the sponsor was most needed – i.e. at the implementation stage.

Recognition and Reward

Finally, in using Spark Groups as a way of accelerating Ignition it is important to remember to reward and recognize their efforts. Public recognition can come in many different forms e.g. a newsletter, a picture in the company paper, a thank you function with the chief executive or more tangible rewards such as money or time off can be extremely helpful to give Ignition a shove forward. If Spark Group efforts are seen to be acknowledged, useful and taken seriously, it is likely to attract other people to Spark Group activity. Organization Ignition needs many Spark Groups at all the different levels of the company.

SPARK GROUPS

What are they?

- They are small groups of people, who come together for a limited time, to focus on a particular problem or issue. They can come from within a particular discipline or be multi-functional.

- Their key aim is to generate energy and momentum for organization Ignition.

How can they help?

- Issues can be tackled with speed

- Numbers of people get involved.

- Different Spark Groups approaching the problem from different angles can provide a range of perspectives.

- They can help to find the cause of problems, resolve significant issues and reach decisions.

- Unusual situations require unusual ways of thinking.

- They can exist in parallel with other organization structures.

Expectations

- Spark Groups are assembled to resolve non-routine, important, critical and urgent issues.

- They must deliver a concrete, well thought-out implementation plan.

- Spark Groups follow through with the implementation plan.

- Spark Groups need to be staffed with competent people and have a sponsor.

When to start

- As soon as a need is recognized.

Who should be part of a Spark Group?

- Those people who are most knowledgeable about the subject or have different points of view.

- Those who are affected by the project and are close to it.

- Someone who has the power to help implement the findings.

- People who can own the problem and contribute to its solution with specific skills and abilities.

- Spark Groups need active, concerned participants, not observers or passengers.

- The Spark Group members need to be persuasive, and able to influence others. They need to have a 'can-do' attitude.

How Many?

- Between six and eight members.

- Add someone temporarily when specialist input is required.

Spark Group Leader

- The Spark Group leader needs to be someone who can move people towards action.

- Someone who is closely in tune with the organization and has 'organization savvy'.

- He/she must have the ability to co-ordinate and synchronize after listening to others.

- The leader must manage the boundaries with the sponsor, with other departments and with the rest of the organization.

- He/she needs effective influencing and interpersonal skills.

Sponsoring a Spark Group

- The sponsor needs to take on the roles of godfather, mentor, troubleshooter, fixer and smoother.

- It is an active role. He/she has to be in contact with the Spark Group leader and the link person with the rest of the organization.

- The sponsor may well initiate a Spark Group.

- He/she needs to be persuasive, have 'political savvy', endurance and determination to ensure that the implementation plan is actioned.

- Any strategic implications arising from the work of the Spark Group need to be fed into other areas of the organization.

- The sponsor can help the Spark group by believing in the project, by providing resources, support and commitment.

- The key tasks for the sponsor are to provide feedback, test out the ideas generated by the Group and modify the plan to ensure its relevance.

- He/she needs to be able to manage the consequences of the Ignition effort.

- Above all he/she must be able to provide reward, recognition and reinforcement for the Spark Group.

Recognition and Reward

- Use different methods of providing recognition and reward for the Spark Group.

- Public recognition will help the Ignition process to spread.

REFERENCES

- *'Eight Big Masters of Innovation'* Fortune Oct 1984.

- *'Independent Business Units'* Inc. April 1984.

- Kidder, T. (1981) *The Soul of a New Machine*, Boston: Little, Brown & Co.

- Car and Driver 1986.

- Waterman, R.H. (1987) *The Renewal Factor*, London: Bantam.

- Peters, T.J. and Waterman, R.H. (1982) *In Search of Excellence*, New York: Harper and Row.

- *'The Un-Manager'* Inc. August 1982.

- Levering, R., Muskowitz, M., and Katz, M. (1984) *The Best Companies to work for in America*, Wokingham: Addison-Wesley.

- *'A Second way to the top'* New York Times Feb 1985.

- Altier, W.J. *'Task Forces – an effective management tool'*, 1986 Sloan Management Review.

- Hastings, C., Bixby, P., Chaudhry-Lawton, R. (1986) *The Superteam Solution*, Aldershot: Gower.

Conclusion

The kind of change that we have called Ignition, requiring as it does fresh ideas, a supportive atmosphere and the energy of Sparks, can greatly benefit an organization. The pay-offs are not by any means organizational alone, as there is plenty of opportunity for fun and personal development in many of the changes facing modern organizations. We also believe that the principle of Ignition can apply to a number of areas outside work, sport being one such example.

Much of our personal and professional satisfaction is gained from helping managers to realize their potential as agents of change. That potential may take some time to surface, as our final example illustrates, but witnessing the process is always rewarding.

We spent some time in discussion with a manager who, some months previously, had attended a training programme, designed to free up creative thought processes, run by a colleague who had since moved on to bigger and better things. During one exercise, he had been asked by our colleague to imagine that he was an egg. He recounted this tale as something which had caused him a lot of confusion at the time but he went on to say that he thought his powers of imagination had now permitted him the flexibility to conceive of himself as being an egg. We teased him by pointing out that this was clearly yesterday's problem and that were our colleague to return he would now require all forward thinking managers to be able to think of themselves as chickens. A look of dismay crossed his face as he realized the implications of what we'd said; but as he walked away he started to flap his elbows in an experimental kind of way and we could swear that we heard the occasional 'cluck'.

Index